One Woman's Awakening from The Nightmare of Spiritual Deception and Bondage

PUSHING
BACK
THE
DARKNESS

JENNIFER REDCAY

WITH BECCA ANDERSON

ISBN 979-8-88616-111-3 (paperback)
ISBN 979-8-88616-112-0 (digital)

Christian Faith Publishing
832 Park Avenue
Meadville, PA 16335
www.christianfaithpublishing.com

Printed in the United States of America

I was absolutely moved by Jennifer's story of her entrapment in this abusive cult. If you are like me at all, you will find yourself angry as the story unfolds, weeping as the love of God reaches out to help her at her job, and rejoicing at the redemptive power of God as she and her family break free from the tyranny of evil. The authors offer practical help and perspective for those who are in, have been in, or are helping those in cults, and they show how that was practically worked out in Jennifer's family.

JIMMY NIMON
Lead Pastor of Lifeway Church

I recommend Jennifer's story to everyone. She acknowledges that she was vulnerable to cultic recruitment because something was missing in her life. Unless we fill our life with God's truth, we too can be misled for lack of discernment.

DAVID HENKE
Founder, Watchman Fellowship, Inc., A
Ministry of Spiritual Discernment

In counseling many abortion-wounded individuals, I have repeatedly heard and felt the devastation swirling in abortion's wake. Jennifer has left an unforgettable mark on my life, not only because of the deception that held her hostage, but more unforgettable is God's search and rescue of one of His beloved daughters. Through Jennifer's courageous healing journey, she experienced God's tender restoration in those broken places. My prayer is that because of her willingness to share vulnerably with us in *Pushing Back the Darkness*, many more will receive courage to look at their own wound and experience the beauty of God's redemption.

CAROL WEAVER

* * *

To my Redeemer, my Restorer, my Lord and Savior, Jesus, who is my reason for living—for without Him I would be nothing. You have turned my mourning into dancing, and I will not be silent (Ps. 30:11-12). To all victims of abuse who are struggling to break free or have broken free, you are the reason for this book. Lastly to my mom, my sister, my niece, my aunt, and my dear friend Afnan: The truth will set you free and, praise God, we are FREE indeed!

JENNIFER REDCAY

* * *

This book is also dedicated to all those wounded by spiritual deception and abuse. May they find peace in Christ at last. And, in memory of Nanci G. Huyser, the gentle grammarian of our critique group. Her fingerprints are all over this book—and my heart.

BECCA ANDERSON

Contents

Note to the Reader

Jennifer Redcay spent nearly a decade in an abusive cult that robbed her of far more than some of the best years of her life. She struggled to regain her footing in the world after escaping the cult, and her goal is to offer warning, comfort and challenge to others in cults.

Becca Anderson had her own brush with spiritual deception, and has spent over 20 years studying cult dynamics, networking with former cultists, and communicating the dangers of cult involvement.

Jennifer's story is a poignant lesson in itself of the importance of discerning God's truth from lies. However, for someone seeking freedom from a cult, whether personally or on behalf of another, additional information can be helpful. Each chapter of this book includes:

- Dramatic descriptions of Jennifer's experiences
- Additional insights and details from Jennifer
- Resources, encouragement, and information by Becca Anderson

The website expands upon and updates the resources listed in these pages. Please visit www.JenniferRedcay.com.

Foreword

One of my favorite promises from God is that He will "give us beauty for ashes." If it were up to me, I would have titled Jennifer Redcay's book Beauty for Ashes instead of Pushing Back the Darkness.

Pushing Back the Darkness combines much needed wisdom concerning recognizing cults together with real healing and wholeness for the victims. It would have been an interesting read just from the account Jennifer gives of a hellish ten years of her life. However, Pushing Back the Darkness is far more than simply recounting her amazing ordeal. It is a testimony to God's redemptive love and grace.

Jennifer is to be thanked for her vulnerable transparency and applauded for refusing to wallow in a "victim" mentality. While acknowledging she was a victim, she also powerfully exemplifies taking responsibility for her poor choices and then making the difficult, but wise, choices in embarking into true freedom.

I can honestly say I am deeply moved by the narrative of her recovery so far. To go from a hopelessly abused and almost captive victim to a happily married woman who adopts a baby, for the sake of love, is a journey of both restoration and victory. Read this book for both the wisdom in recognizing and possibly helping cult victims but also for the sheer joy of knowing Jennifer's story.

MARC A. DUPONT
Conference speaker and author of Toxic
Churches and other books
Markdupontministries.com

Introduction

The same dog-eared posters clutter the bulletin boards of the Department of Motor Vehicles waiting room, the same cloud of mingled human odors presses down from the acoustic tile ceiling. I slide lower in the fiberglass chair, trying not to snag my jeans on the notched edge. Like I did last time. I keep my chin down in case someone monitoring the security cameras recognizes me. My heart flutters each time someone is called forward.

"Number 855." The clerk peers over the top of her reading glasses, her eyes dull, her hair somewhat askew. If she's served 854 other people today, I can understand why. The damp paper in my hand has transferred its grunge to my palm, but I remember the number and stand, approach the desk, and slide my paperwork and money toward her.

My hands shake underneath the counter's edge.

"Replacement license. What happened to the first one?" She begins punching keys on a grimy keyboard even as she interrogates me.

The first one? What did I say about the first one? I mumble a reply that even I can't really understand.

Her fingers pause midstroke as her eyebrows descend like twin express elevators. "What the—" Her posture straightens and her fingers fly clickety-click across the keys. Piercing gray eyes drill into me. "What's going on here?"

Caught! She's caught me! I draw in a ragged breath, my trembling hands locking together at my waist as if already manacled. Finally.

"Says here you've done this a few times now."

"Um… I'm just…you know, going through a phase." I laugh, but it sounds more like someone strangling a parrot. "I can't seem to keep hold of stuff. I've been distracted. Lots going on in my life. Really crazy. I'm trying to get a better handle on things, I promise…" Now that I'm talking, I can't seem to stop.

"Nine times since July. *Nine?*" The express elevators have gone back up to the observation deck, disappearing into her hairline.

Please. Please, just ask me. Stop me. Don't give it to me! This could be the end of it. Please.

She sighs, and the paperwork shimmies on the desk. Her meaty hand slaps down to keep it in place. "You're not selling these to illegals, are you?"

"What?" I'm dumbfounded. That possibility never occurred to me. "No, of course not. I'm just…clumsy." My face is hot, and I want to wipe the dampness from my upper lip but dare not ungrip my hands.

She gives me a long, appraising stare. A cough from the waiting people behind me jars loose her right shoulder, which twitches in a shrug. "Whatever. Hope I'm not on the road when you are, if you're that. clumsy." In slow motion, her hand picks up the metal stamper, clunks it three times on the paperwork, and then her other hand slides it all back to me. She smirks and nods me to the next waiting station. "I'm sure you know where to go."

For a moment I'm rooted to the stained linoleum. I imagine begging her to take the papers back. Imploring her to dig deeper. As my spirit collapses inside me, I reach for the paperwork and shuffle deeper into the DMV office.

My earlier, regurgitated photo will look out from the license with optimism. I don't look like it any more, my sad brown eyes ringed with deepening circles. The eyes are the window of the soul, they say. I wonder what someone looking through my windows can see. Why don't they look?

Can they see my terror? The shame of what happens in those motel rooms? The purging of my belongings and clothes after each session-necessitating this ninth trip to the DMV since July? A close look might reveal the flickering image of Seth, his brows drawn, his mouth down-turned in anger, his hands…

Nobody looks at anything except my paperwork.

Seth's counting on that.

The license is still warm when the girl hands it to me. My hands are ice cold and greedy to suck the heat from the plastic. I examine it, wondering where the girl with the tangled brown curls and cheerful dimple has gone.

I have a license to drive a car. Where do I apply for a license to run my life?

The slick new I.D. slips into my wallet. No snags. No wear and tear. It probably won't have time to develop any, either, before I'm back to apply for its next sibling. Better that than letting the demons jump from the motel room to the license I used to rent it, and into my life. This one is still demon-free. I'll enjoy it while it lasts.

Outside, I turn the key in the ignition and creep from the parking lot on my way back home. To the house Seth assigned to me when I joined his group.

It's all the license I have…

* * *

Meet Jennifer: nice person, ex-cult member…

I NEVER STOOD ON A STREET CORNER WITH A SIGN AROUND MY NECK, saying, "Will join cult if asked." Yet looking back over nine years of bondage and deception, I now recognize the sign was there whether I realized it or not. Others saw it, and that was enough.

Nobody joins a cult in a single day. There are preparations that must be made, groundwork laid in order to make the decisions that come later seem both logical and inevitable. Seeds were planted deep in my soul that burst to the surface when the nurturing warmth of the cult leader's attention caused them to germinate and grow. I labored side by side with those who deceived me in order to coax fruit from the plants that crowded my heart and spirit. But the fruit was bitter, poisonous, malignant. By then, I had no skill to inspect it before I consumed it and started on a new crop.

It's easy to think that only stupid people get caught up in cults, a comfort to think they must all be weak-minded, flabby-willed, ignorant of basic psychology and lacking in biblical knowledge. Such thinking has gotten more smart, normal, God-seeking people into cults than anything else. Denial can be a powerful thing. Once you're captured, shame and guilt keep you pinned in place like a butterfly in a museum collection-beautiful, but dead.

I surrendered over nine precious years of what most people would consider the best part of my life, from my mid-twenties to my mid-thirties, to people who controlled my every action, decisions, even thoughts. How could I be so foolish? Why didn't I walk away, before I had to run for my life?

Journey with me as I travel down the corridors of my life in search of answers. *What made me so vulnerable to the lies? And, more important, How can I avoid ever becoming absorbed in a cult again?* My story is the same as hundreds of thousands of people who also took a wrong turn into spiritual deception. You may know some of them. They will probably never admit it. That, too, is part of the pattern of deception. I want to throw open the doors of my own dark journey to allow the fresh breeze of honesty and truth to keep even one more soul from following a path into spiritual bondage.

Take my hand. It's dark, but Jesus is carrying the light for us, and light overcomes darkness. I was trapped in darkness for so long; it's time I pushed back.

Chapter I

Heart Stealer

"Stick 'em up!" I shout, brandishing my thumb-and-forefinger six-shooter. The tall, lanky man in coveralls jumps at my voice, and his hands spring above his head. His huge, black shadow reaches right past me, as if it's going to tickle me from behind if I'm not careful.

My father's eyes crinkle in a funny way. "Don't shoot, little lady. I'm no outlaw."

"Sorry, Daddy." I holster my finger. "I thought you was Bad Bart." The wind ruffles my hair and the perfect California sun toasts my eyelids. I squint to see Daddy better. The sun is right behind his head, and his face is in shadow.

I thought he'd scoop me up in his big arms and toss me into the air, even if I am the sheriff for today. The badge on my cowgirl outfit says so. I put my hand on top of my hat to keep it from blowing off, and then tighten the strap under my chin. Daddy is behaving like a bad guy in the westerns, shuffling his feet and not looking at me.

He jingles the keys in his pocket. An excited bubble rises in my chest.

"We goin' to the store, Daddy?" My brown boots tap in glee on the sidewalk. I jump onto the big piece of driftwood next to the porch, clap, and smile.

"Not today, Pumpkin." The sun is still bright but feels like it's fading. The light breeze of the moment before turns into a gust and whines around the far corner of the garage. I hate that sound, and it draws my eye for a ghost-wary glance.

Daddy's car crouches on the driveway, facing the street. Behind it, a funny orange thing like a horse trailer rocks slightly from the sudden wind. He brought it home last night. He hasn't shown me inside yet.

I point to the trailer. "Can we look in the box? Last night you said we could."

His big, brown hand comes out of his jeans pocket and sweeps through his hair. I brace myself. Whenever Daddy touches his hair, he's about to tell me something that doesn't always turn out to be true. He swipes at his eyes with the back of his hand. "Stupid dust in the air," he mumbles.

The baby cries from the kitchen. I look and see Momma and my little sister in the doorway at the back of the garage. The screen makes it hard to see, but a shadow of Momma wipes her eyes; the baby isn't the only one crying.

With a frown, I turn back to Daddy. My hat blows off my head and its cord snags around my neck. I let it bump on my back, my wild curls almost blinding me to the single tear on his face.

He sighs and his shoulders sag. Shaking his head from side to side he comes over and sits on the big driftwood log. He braces his hands on his knees and gazes out on the neighborhood. Down the street kids play with a Frisbee. A dog barks and chases one of the boys. A man starts a lawn mower. I smell hamburgers cooking somewhere.

Daddy turns toward me. As I stand on the log our faces are almost even, and I look deep into his wet eyes. My hands creep down, and each take a big handful of my cowgirl skirt, back behind me where he can't see. I clench tight.

"I've got to go on a little trip, Sweetheart." He blinks several times. "That trailer has some of my stuff in it that I might need. I have to finish up my training so I can be a vet." He pushes the curls out of my face. "You remember how we talked about taking care of all the horses and ponies?"

I nod. But somehow I know this isn't about Black Beauty or Silver Blaze. The handfuls of skirt become damp in my grip.

"I'll be gone about a month, maybe a little longer." He looks at me like he's not sure I understand. "When I get back, we'll play and talk just like always, okay?"

The baby cries louder. The sound recedes as Momma moves away from the door. Daddy stands up abruptly, saying something about the dust again.

Without looking at my face, he pats me on the head, crosses the lawn, rounds the front of the car, and opens the driver's door. He waves, more or less in my direction, but his eyes are on the street. He slides behind the wheel and starts the car in one motion. The door slams; the car and trailer begin to roll forward.

He's getting away! I make a quick reach for my gun, only to find my holster as empty as my heart.

Bad Bart drives off with my dreams and my heart locked in his trailer.

* * *

"Where's my daddy?"

THE FIRST QUESTIONS PEOPLE ASK ME when they learn I spent nearly ten years in a cult is, "Why did you get into it? What were you looking for?" Everyone who joins a cult has a different answer, but I know I was looking for my father. He left my life one sunny day when I was four, and though he returned two years later, our family broke apart and I grew up fifteen hundred miles from him. Confused and uncertain in her second marriage, my mother joined the cult before I became involved. I think we were both looking for Daddy.

Cults are parental in nature. The authority figure in the group tells everyone what to do, when and how to do it, and hands out punishment if his orders aren't followed. When punishment becomes necessary, it's always couched in terms of being what is best for the cult member and said to be done out of love, just as a parent explains a well-deserved spanking. I hungered for a father I struggled to remember. Desperate for someone to "finish" raising me, I craved an authority who could set my feet on the right path.

I was wide open and vulnerable to a manipulator.

After my father left us, we remained in California for a few years. My mother became very ill and unable to work or care for my sister and me. Her family stepped in to rescue us. They moved us back to Central Pennsylvania, where we lived in a house a mile and a half from my grandparents that they purchased for us. My mother rented the house from them for a nominal amount. Mom recovered and was able to go back to work, so my sister and I spent each day after school at our grandparents' house until she got home. Life became stable, but something was still missing.

■ I hungered for a father I struggled to remember. ■

My mother did everything she could to make up for my father's absence. We had lots of times filled with laughter and fun. My favorite memories are times spent in summer at a beach condo our grandparents owned. We'd play in the ocean, run the boardwalk, and wear ourselves out with fresh sea air. One magical night my mother waited until my sister fell asleep and then got me out of bed. The two of us returned to the boardwalk alone and rode all the attractions my sister was too young to ride. We giggled as the music and lights danced around us in a joyful cloud. We believed in God in our household, so when the longing for a husband and father grew too much, we turned to Him. My mother, sister, and I made a list of all the things we felt were important in the man who we hoped would complete our family. We prayed before bedtime each night for him to come into our lives. In the end, a man she met through work caught our mother's eye. She assumed "Ed" was God's answer to her prayers and didn't check directly with the Lord. After a bumpy courtship, they married.

Ed fought the two sides of the bi-polar teeter-totter as best he could. When he was stable, times were good. He was kind and steady and we could depend on him, as we'd longed to do. But sometimes manic phases got the better of him—weeks of frantic activity, enormous projects begun and never finished, a household turned upside down. The thrill rides on the boardwalk seemed tame by comparison. The hole in our lives, imperfectly filled, yawned afresh and threatened to pull us all into its depths.

* * *

The pain of life can drive people in directions they'd never take in normal circumstances. Many people look back on the beginning of their cult experience and recognize they were vulnerable to be approached by the group because of the turmoil in their lives. My mother heard about the group we all eventually joined from her sister, who had met "Seth" (not his real name) at a bookstore he and his wife owned. Aunt Carolyn had gone in seeking a greeting card for her son who was leaving to go on a mission trip. She was upset about her son's impending departure, and her husband was very ill as well, which added to her stress level.

The bookstore owner approached her and asked what she was looking for. She explained, and suddenly he gave Carolyn a "word of knowledge" about herself. He told her that God loved her, saw her pain, and was pleased with her efforts to help everyone and love everyone around her. It was very comforting and affirming. Each time she went to the store, the man slowly drew her into his sphere of influence by giving additional encouraging words of knowledge.

My aunt was serious about seeking God—as many people who end up in religious cults are. The general pew-sitter doesn't get caught up in aberrant groups because he or she is content. Those who look for a deeper experience are vulnerable to being misled if they aren't carefully studying the Bible and hearing godly counsel from stronger Christians, pastors and friends. Carolyn's inability to find a congregation that shared her passion kept her moving from church to church, never putting down roots. Hungry for a deeper spirituality, she tried to seek God on her own, and asked Him to send someone to her who really knew Him. The bookstore owner seemed to be her answer.

My mother's difficult marriage encouraged her to draw strength from her relationship with her sister, rather than her husband. She became intrigued when her sister began talking about Seth. Without solid Bible knowledge, my mother was unable to discern when Seth's interpretation of Scripture departed from the truth.

My younger sister became another family casualty. Janice had led a wild lifestyle for a time and got into drugs but finally began to realize she needed God. Impressionable, she became an easy catch for Seth.

When I first heard the teaching that so excited my family members, it made me uneasy. I was no theological giant—in fact, I had only recently turned back to God myself and attended church sporadically. But alarm bells went off in my head. They called the teaching "deliverance ministry," which seemed to focus on identifying sins and demons in people or situations and then casting them out. I wanted nothing to do with it. All the charismatic gifts described in the Bible, like speaking in tongues, healing or prophecy, made me uncomfortable. This appeared to be along those lines. I gave the group and its teachings a second look because of the positive difference it seemed to be making in the lives of the people I loved. Suddenly my sister completely abandoned her former lifestyle and focused her life on God. My mother and aunt found new peace.

■ Alarm bells went off in my head. ■

Seth himself did not appeal to me at all. I spoke to him on the phone once while trying to help my sister sell her car. He spoke in a very seductive tone that raised the hair on the back of my neck. I shuddered. "That guy gives me the creeps."

He and his wife, "Rhoda" (not her real name), had decided my sister should sell her car and move to California to extend the ministry there. When it came time for her to leave, we had a farewell dinner at their store after hours. I was suffering from carpal tunnel syndrome at the time, and I removed my braces before going to the dinner. I didn't want them to put their hands on me and pray over me. Something about them frightened me; not allowing them to have a reason to pray over me kept them at a distance.

Seth broke through to me eventually after he gave one of his "words of knowledge" about my future. He said I had a special call on my life, and that my husband would be like Gideon and do great things for God. Hungry for acceptance, validation, and spiritual growth, this proclamation excited me. He went on to say, however, that I had an idol in my life—something I loved and wanted more than God.

I desperately wanted to be a mother. He offered to pray with me and break the idol's bondage and cast it out of me. I wept through the deliverance prayer session because it felt like I was giving up a dream, but I let him do it anyway. After that first session I began waking up in the middle of the night with page numbers from the Bible in my mind. I'd open the Bible, scan the page, and find verses related to either the Israelites coming out of bondage in Egypt or about idols.

Something must have really happened to me when I was prayed over. I sensed I was changing, growing, and it was exciting. This confirmation and sudden understanding made me realize what had attracted my family members to this ministry, and I began to seek deliverance counseling from Seth and Rhoda.

■ I sensed I was changing, growing, and it was exciting. ■

I was twenty-six when I first got involved in the cult. I was also married. John wasn't a believer, though we married in a church. He didn't like the fact that this new interest made me less fun to be around. I wouldn't go drinking with him anymore and, according to him, spent too much time with Seth and Rhoda at their store after hours when they practiced their ministry.

One day Seth said I had a generational curse on my family related to incest. He said he had a word from God that my father had molested me when I was a small child. I didn't remember any such thing, but his firm conviction swayed me. I went home and told my husband.

He exploded. "I've had enough of this, Jen! Either you get your head on straight and we get back to normal, or you leave."

"I can't help it if I was abused! Seth says—"

"I've heard what Seth says from morning to night around here. I don't care what he says. How do you even know if what he says is true? No matter whether he's right or wrong, I want him out of our marriage, or we're through."

John was deeply concerned about the group and the things I was being told. He took the Bible I was using at the time and went to see his brother's pastor. The pastor listened to what he described, looked at my notes, and said it sounded like a cult to him. "Once people get into these things, they usually don't come out of them. There's probably nothing you can say or do that will turn her back."

Though I didn't know much Scripture, I had read the passage that says if a believer is married to an unbeliever, the only way a separation can occur that God will accept is if the unbeliever leaves the believer. Seth and Rhoda prayed with me, asking God that, if the marriage was against His will, my husband would leave.

I stayed, and eventually John left. I then felt free to follow my family into the group and did so. It never occurred to me to question the initial "prophecy" Seth had pronounced over my life, regarding my husband. Since I now had no husband, the so-called prophecy proved false. Had I understood Scripture better, it might have been a stone in my path to trip me up and make me think twice. Instead, I continued in willful ignorance.

* * *

Where was God in all this? Why didn't He stop me if I was seeking Him? Like others who have been in cults, I can look back and see the roadblocks God put up to turn me away from danger—but I insisted on going around, jumping over, or crawling under them. Several times He sent friends and family members to dissuade me.

I had two coworkers who were Christians. Each morning we had a three-way call to pray together about our day, the company, and other needs. As I told them the things I'd learned from Seth, they became alarmed and gently tried to explain that his teachings were not biblical. My sister-in-law and her sister came to talk with me about my crumbling marriage. They urged me to go for counseling with my husband rather than giving up. They said I was not being submissive to the Bible by letting the group take precedence over my marriage. I refused their counsel.

Even my mother, already involved with Seth and Rhoda, was uneasy about my getting involved in their group. Seth had urged her to divorce my stepfather when she underwent counseling for deliverance. Though she moved in with my aunt, it upset her that a "man of God" would also counsel me to leave my husband. He also told us to cut ties to other family members who didn't understand the new truths we were learning. This didn't square with what little she knew from the Bible and raised doubts in her mind about our involvement. I was too far down the path by that point to turn back, however. Seth limited our contact with each other, to prevent her fears from being voiced.

An increase in my excitement concerning my future according to Seth coincided with the discouragement of friends and family members. He indicated I would be part of a great ministry, something the world needed desperately. I began getting words of knowledge for other people, and that thrilled me. I felt special, and these prophecies confirmed in my mind that there was a call on my life. That was hugely attractive to me, more so because of my disarrayed life.

One night, I had a vivid dream. In it, an enormous snake lay coiled outside my house. Persistent, it pressed and sought until it found a way to get in and slithered through a window. It bit me on the leg. The pain was so horrible it woke me from the dream. The next day I discovered two small marks on my leg. Looking back, I wonder if it wasn't God trying to tell me I had been bitten by "the snake," His enemy, Satan, and I needed to get away.

Seth always had an interpretation for any dream, and he was very convincing. Despite my initial repugnance, I began to find him charismatic and persuasive. He seemed to know so much Scripture, and I certainly did not. I didn't realize he took things out of context and twisted them to fit his own purposes. I naively accepted everything he said. He seemed to have answers to the questions I asked, could see right into my soul, and projected great confidence in his own calling and God's purpose for all our lives.

I finally had a father to take me by the hand and guide me.

■ Thinking It Through…■

Red Flags of Spiritually Abusive Groups

Every cult is as different as the people in it, but many of the warning signs are similar. If you or someone you know fits the profile listed below, step back and seriously consider what is going on.

Characteristics of a Spiritually Abusive Group

1. Claim a superior status with God—The leader(s) of the group flatters the followers by telling them they are unique, special, chosen, etc., to fulfill God's will and that no one else can do what they are doing.
2. Focus on the leader's position of authority—Leaders claim a "chain of command" or "delegated authority" from God where followers submit to their superiors without question.
3. Provide no accountability for leaders—The leader allows his adoring followers to elevate him to a pedestal where it is considered a sin to question him. The leader can impose his will with little resistance because whatever he says is considered to be coming from God.
4. Try to control followers' time and sources of information—Groups keep the followers so busy they don't have time to reflect on any issues they notice. Information from other religious sources may be characterized as "spiritual pornography" unworthy of attention; information from ex-members is "apostate literature." Without good information it is more difficult to organize dissent.
5. Close followers off from outsiders—Those outside the group are viewed as either future converts or people to be avoided. Potential converts are tolerated conditionally until recruitment. Others are avoided because they can cor-

rupt one's thinking and turn them against God and His organization.

6. Followers put on a performance treadmill—The idea is planted that the follower will gain God's blessing by how well he performs in the group's program. There is never a time when he has done enough, however. Job, family, friends, personal time, and interests can all be sacrificed for the group.

7. Emphasize conformity to legalistic rules—The leader says God wants obedience to the rules or commands the leader espouses. The boundary between God's commandments and man's commandments is obscured or denied in high control groups. These rules can become tests of loyalty for the follower's devotion.

8. Using guilt and fear to manipulate compliance—The most insidious tools in the controller's toolbox are guilt and fear. The leader wants his followers to think poorly of themselves. At the same time, he holds out the ideal of spiritual peace and tranquility to those who succeed in a spiritual walk defined by the leadership as being in compliance with their rules, standards, and expectations.

9. Blame misfortune on lack of faith—Whether it is disease, an accident, emotional collapse, or any other problem, the follower would not have had this problem if he had more faith. It is also common for the leaders to shame people before the whole group, even naming names.

10. Wound people spiritually and emotionally—The cumulative effect of these control methods is serious emotional and spiritual wounding. When the confused, disillusioned, hurting individual begins to actively search for help, he sets in motion a whole new set of control methods.

11. Shut off discussion about forbidden subjects—Questioning the leader or group is forbidden. The follower who questions will be forced to submit and humbly accept the dictates of the leader or not submit and either leave or be expelled from the group.

12. Label those who dissent—Those who ask too many questions will be labeled by the leader(s) as troublemakers, or worse. They may even be publicly shamed. The purpose of labeling is to put the person in a category that everyone agrees is to be avoided.
13. Label former members as unspiritual—Former members must be kept away from the members in good standing, often done by the threat of discipline (including excommunication) for anyone talking with an ex-member.

(Adapted with permission from Watchman Fellowship, Inc., The News and Views, Vol. 11, No. 20, 2009.)

If a ministry, group or church is biblically sturdy, it will bear up under scrutiny. If you feel uneasy even considering asking questions about what you are being taught or what you are involved in, that is a warning flag in itself.

Legitimate ministries never mind sincere questions asked in a loving and honest way.

So, question. Search. Study. Your spiritual life and destiny may depend on it.

Chapter 2

Clean

My eyes shoot open as pale dawn creeps between the blinds. My hand fumbles for the pad of paper and pen on the bedside table even before I slide my feet over the side of the bed. Silence fills the house. The scratching of my pen on the page startles me, as my hand flies feverishly across the first page. Every detail of my dreams spills onto the white sheets, shaping the day ahead as much as they have the night just past.

I write for almost half an hour, pausing only to close my eyes and force each color, sound, and image before it fades.

I have to get it all. All. All.

The clock reads half past six when I put aside the pad and dart into the bathroom to shower and dress. I must be ready when the phone rings. Have to be ready.

My hair hangs in dripping strands when the uneasy silence is shattered by loud ringing. I take a deep breath and pick up the receiver.

"Yes." No need to ask who is calling. No need for pleasantries. Only the need to express my willingness to obey.

"Tell me about it." His smooth voice runs like liquid into my ear, close and hot as a whispered breath. "Everything."

I look at my notes and start describing my dream. "I'm in my car driving to work. It's raining, and the windshield wipers won't work." My trembling vibrates my voice. I take a breath. "I peer through the glass but can't see well. I am terrified I'll hit something..." Sweat trickles down my back, undoing the good of my recent shower.

"Ah, that old demon." He sounds disappointed. "Your pride is rearing its ugly, disgusting, God-hating head again. Why do you suppose that is?"

I swallow hard and my heart thuds. As always, my mind races to guess what answer he wants. It doesn't bode well to start out so badly. We have pages yet to go through.

* * *

Two hours after it began, the interrogation ends. Ink blotches every inch of my already-messy pages, scribbled notes swim before my tearful eyes. So much work to do today!

"I'd begun to think you were making progress toward the calling God has on your life, but after hearing all this, I can see you're not." The catch in his voice wrenches a sob from my throat.

"I've lost track of the number of demons your dreams harbor, much less all the ones in your house. We'll be coming over this evening, and you know I can't come in if you haven't dealt with all of them properly. I will stand at the door and knock. If you hear my voice, it will mean you've put the demons out, and I'll come in and dine with you. If not, well, we may need to reconsider your role in the coming great work of God."

"I'll take care of them! I will. I swear! They'll be gone before you come. I'm so sorry." I've slid off the chair into a heap on the floor and want nothing more than to hide under the rag rug. But I don't have time for that. I've got work to do.

"See that you do." The line goes dead, like my heart.

* * *

I start at the top of the first page. The demon of my pride jumps off the page at me, and I must bind it with a quick prayer. "Father, I put this pride of mine under subjection to Your will. Purge it out of me, bind it, cast it away from me, keep me from allowing it back into my life to taunt me and injure those around me. Cleanse me, O God, and make me pure again."

The next image included a red cardinal circling my head.

"A sexual symbol, a sign of your evil heart," he hissed over the phone.

I ruthlessly grapple with the demon inherent in the symbol and wrestle it to the ground, begging God to remove it from my heart, my mind, my spirit. I feel no release. I go to the next demon's name on the list of my nocturnal wanderings. The list clogs four pages.

* * *

It is noon when I put aside my pen and rip the dream pages into small bits. I flush the pile of bits down the toilet, glad to get them out of the house. My shoulders ache from tension; my hand is cramped from holding the pen and crossing off the dozens of demons I let into the house in one night's dreams. At least these have been sent packing.

Hungry, I head into the kitchen for something to eat. I see demons in every corner, snickering at me and ready to resume the fight. I begin another list of demons to deal with before Seth and Rhoda can enter my home.

I open a cupboard, wishing for coffee. I slam the door and pray God will take away the demon of sophistication at the same time He deals with the demon of laziness, inherent in my need for caffeine. I settle for water, but only after blessing the liquid as it runs from the tap, to keep any demons in the city water supply from entering my house when I'm not looking.

Moving from room to room through the rest of the day, I do battle with every demon I can name. They seem to come in legions—brothers, cousins, relatives. Perhaps demons are incapable of traveling alone. I pray and weep and draw a shield between me and them, careful to stay alert and remember where they've hidden in my life in the past.

Once I'm done with the house, my ears catch the tunes of birds outside. "There are demons in those birds," Seth has said. Different birds have different kinds of demons. I must discern what kinds of birds they are so I can pray for God to ban them and their demons from my yard.

* * *

Just before Seth and Rhoda are due to arrive, I look outside, checking the yard one last time. My heart sinks.

I haven't gotten the mail!

I begin to shake. Do I leave it in the box and pretend I forgot? Or should I go out and get it—knowing I'll have to spend time praying against the demons that can leap from each piece of mail into my house. I won't know if any are out there until I check the box. They could try to jump on Seth.

Maybe there's nothing there today.

Or maybe there's an offer from a credit card company carrying the demon of greed, and right under it another notice that I'm late on a bill, hauling a demon of worry and fear right along with the stamp.

I glance up the road. No sign of a car yet. Can I make it to the box, check it, and deal with any demons I find before Seth arrives? I bolt out the door...

* * *

Keeping the devil at bay

THE GROUP WE WERE PART OF focused on discovering any conceivable way demons could attack people, and prayed against them specifically. On the surface, this sounds like a noble thing to do. The end result, however, is that demons became the sole focus of our thoughts and efforts, not God.

I had never really thought about demons and their influence on people before I got involved in the cult. Once I joined the group, it was all I thought about. I was free to do so because I was set up in a house, told to quit my job and spent the first year in the group living alone and interacting only with Seth and Rhoda. They paid my rent, utilities, and car payment. I was asked to get credit card advances to contribute to their expenses.

■ Demons became the sole focus of our thoughts and efforts, not God. ■

A typical day involved spending time with the two of them. They taught me specific prayers to pray for any situation. I wrote down all the details of my dreams first thing each morning and then spent hours going through the details to find the demons behind them. Everything had significance. The color red was a sign of lust. Different animals meant different things. Seth could explain it all and pin the name of a demon on each detail. Once the demons had been named, I cast them out of myself one by one, ripped up the pages, and destroyed them. The whole time I was in the cult, I experienced dreams that were vivid and memorable. This meant I had much work to do every day.

We prayed all the time, but not like I do today. We didn't praise God; we tried to contain demons. Seth felt he had special powers and prayed two hours each morning over the earth, the universe, and prophecies that came to him. He taught me prayers to say to keep from being connected to another person (breaking "soul ties"), words to whisper when leaving anywhere or if someone called on the telephone, to keep demons from following or attaching to me. We prayed that whatever demons were involved would be sent back on the people who introduced them to us.

If I ran into an old friend, it meant I had left doors open to the past, and I was required to bind all familiar spirits and cast them away. I became afraid to go anywhere for fear of running into people I knew. When I did go out, I walked with my head down and avoided eye contact. I did not touch anyone, since I'd been told demons could jump from them to me.

We spent hours watching movies—everything from Disney to pornography. I was shocked. Seth's explanation was that Satan reveals himself in movies. He gives away his demonic names and hides them in drama and science fiction, horror, comedy, and especially pornography. We also watched the *Matrix* movies repeatedly, since Seth felt he had a special call on his life like the main character in the movies, and he and Rhoda thought their bodies would be changed (as is talked about in the films).

■ We spent hours watching movies— everything from Disney to pornography. ■

After we watched a movie, we'd have to make lists of all the demons we spotted. Then we did what Seth called "the gamut." This involved casting out every demon that had come into being through the movie. The gamut took two hours after the movie was over—and we'd watch two films a night. Sometimes we were up until dawn.

It's easy to say, "If demons came in through the movies, why watch them?" At the time we were engaged in these rituals, it seemed like worthwhile spiritual work. Seth said we all had a part in a very special ministry to purge ourselves of every demon and then take back the earth for the Lord. If you hear something like that enough times, while deprived of input from other people, you begin to believe it.

Everything I did (or didn't do) was related to keeping demons under control. Seth first allowed me to wear a bit of makeup, then forbid it, saying it encouraged the demon of vanity. My clothes had to be conservative and in muted tones. Red, purple, and yellow were forbidden. Skirts were forbidden, as they represented a tunnel for demons to attack women. We wore slacks, regardless of the weather, never shorts. If we wore capri pants, we also had to wear knee-high pantyhose so there was no uncovered skin.

Coffee was forbidden because it carried the demon of sophistication. Chocolate and sweets were out—they had an aphrodisiac effect. (Oddly, we could indulge in them if we were out, but not at home.)

Music had to be pre-approved by Seth. I purchased many CDs of Christian music at the bookstore he and Rhoda ran, but every year he would go through my collection and weed it down. Each time he discarded an artist's music, he had a specific reason for doing so.

By the end, there were no CDs left that were acceptable, out of the hundreds I'd owned.

Books got the same treatment, with some that were initially "approved" being forbidden later.

Though we watched dozens of movies, I wasn't allowed to have a television set at my house. We'd watch movies at Seth and Rhoda's home. Yet they'd take me to a video arcade (at least in the beginning) and let me play. It was the only entertainment I got; there was no other time to have fun.

After my first year living alone, Seth allowed my mother and me to share a house. This should have eased the burden of all the restrictions, but we were forbidden to speak to one another. We could not eat in the same room (though we broke that rule quite a bit) and had assigned seats in the living room. This was to protect us from whatever demons we each might pick up. If you sat in someone else's seat, their demons could get hold of you, too. Seth determined the layout of the furniture.

We had separate bathrooms, but the only shower in the house was in my mother's bathroom. I anointed it every day to prevent anything on her from attaching itself to me. I was frantic if someone sat in my car seat and had specific prayers to cleanse it.

No flowers could be planted outside the house because there were demons in the soil. When we moved from one house to another, we were required to rip out all the plants in the yard and put in grass seed. Bushes and even trees had to be removed because birds would get too close to the house, and they were infested with demons.

If we broke rules, Seth always found out somehow. It was eerie. Punishments were harsh. He said God hated us. The only chance we had to avoid hell was to come into repentance before Jesus returns, and we'd been given the opportunity to do that through this ministry. We'd been specially chosen for our work, and if we walked away from it, there would be no chance for us to avoid God's wrath and condemnation.

■ If we broke rules, Seth always found out somehow. ■

It was eerie. ■

It's very hard to describe all this. To read it here in stark ink is to admit the foolishness of our trust in Seth. It shows how immature we were as Christians. What could possibly make me stay in such an environment?

For one thing, Seth was very persuasive when he described the work we were doing. It felt like we had this unbelievable purpose. We were part of something huge. God was going to use our ministry to accomplish something special, and it was a heady experience to be chosen. We all had to work harder than anyone else in the world to be cleansed and prepared to do the work God called us to. Seth said we were blessed with more knowledge than others, more power, more insight. It generated an elite feeling and a spiritual pride.

God chose me for whatever reason and I've got to do whatever I've got to do just to be part of this. The allure of a thought like that is powerful.

Seth was going to be used to bring God's ultimate plan into place. I wanted to be right there with him when it happened. He said he could use me to help, but only if I lived by the rules and disciplined myself to be ready.

I had an enormous need to be accepted and special. For the first time I felt someone was taking care of me, loving me. Seth and Rhoda would call early in the morning to see how I was. In the middle of the night, Seth might call and say, "The Lord told me to call you. Are you okay?" This frequently happened when I was having a bad dream, and he'd help me interpret it and calm me down. It made me feel safe. I thought he was in tune with God and I didn't want to be away from him. I came to worship the ground he walked on and wanted to make him proud; I'd do whatever it took to earn that.

When Seth and Rhoda told me to call them Father and Mom, I did. It hurt my mother terribly to have her daughter call her by her first name, but my need for a family—no matter how strange—was bottomless. I had no idea how bad it could get.

■ Thinking It Through...■

Eyes to See

The heart of the issue in Jennifer's experience of being drawn into a cult was her lack of discernment about the things the leader was telling her. It sounded so great to hear that he thought she had a "special ministry." Without the tools of biblical discernment, she was unable to separate truth from lies.

What is discernment?

Bible teacher John MacArthur has written, "In its simplest definition, discernment is nothing more than the ability to decide between truth and error, right and wrong. Discernment is the process of making careful distinctions in our thinking about truth. In other words, the ability to think with discernment is synonymous with the ability to think biblically."[1]

How can you discern truth from error and keep from falling under the alluring spell of unbiblical ideas?

- Read the Bible for yourself. Jennifer was a casual Christian. She was not familiar with the Bible and was therefore vulnerable to the leader twisting the Scriptures to suit his own purposes. Biblical knowledge doesn't come overnight or from casual reading. It takes work. Read it systematically and regularly. If you are confronted with something that sounds like it "might" be from the Bible, or someone makes claims and backs them up with Bible verses, talk to someone more knowledgeable about the Bible (a friend, pastor, etc.) if you do not feel you have the ability yet to properly check out what you're being told.
- Don't be afraid to question what is said. When the apostle Paul was preaching in various cities, he praised the people of Berea because they didn't take what he said at face value. They spent diligent time comparing it with the Scriptures

they had and learned for themselves he was telling the truth. Anyone who insists you take his or her interpretation and not question it should set off alarm bells. Ask. Dig. Go to those who know more if you need to.

- Test those who say they speak for God. In 1 John 4:1, the Bible says, "Do not believe every spirit, but test the spirits to see whether they are from God; because many false prophets have gone out into the world." You approach a salesperson with a degree of skepticism, expecting to hear things that might not be as good as they are described. It is even more vital to maintain healthy caution with regard to people who try to "sell" you ideas that sound biblical but may not be. If what is being said is true, it will stand up to scrutiny, and over time.

- Listen to the Holy Spirit inside you. Jennifer's initial reaction to the group leader was negative. Only when he began telling her things that fed her ego did she soften toward him. Listen to the warning voice inside you when it tells you to pull back, and think things through. If you are a Christian, you have the Holy Spirit of God living inside you, and can ask for wisdom and guidance. You won't hear an audible voice but will often feel a pull in one direction or another. James 1:5 says, "But if any of you lacks wisdom, let him ask of God, who gives to all generously and without reproach, and it will be given to him." If something you hear or are taught makes you uncomfortable, ask God to reveal the truth to you. Then give Him time and quiet to do so, reading the Word.

- Look at the fruit. Jesus said we could judge the soundness of a tree by the kind of fruit it produced:

"For there is no good tree which produces bad fruit, nor, on the other hand, a bad tree which produces good fruit" (Luke 6:43). What fruit does the life of the person you are listening to exhibit? The fruits of the Spirit are love, joy, peace, patience, kindness, goodness, faithfulness, gentleness, and self-control (Galatians 5:22-23). If the doctrines you are hearing do not lead to this kind of fruit, don't consume them. In Jennifer's case, the doctrines she was taught led to fear, self-loathing, exhaustion, inferiority and depression. The leader himself exhibited pride, control (over others, not himself), anger, violence, and an attraction to ungodly things. If the fruit is bad, the tree it comes from should be avoided.

We can all use some help discerning the truth from lies at times. Whether you are currently struggling with something, or simply want to be prepared, make a list of two or three more mature Christians you could go to for discerning, godly counsel. If you are in a group you have concerns about, these counselors should be outside the group in order to give you clear perspective. Believers who have wrestled out issues on their own are willing to share what they've learned, so don't be afraid to ask.

Chapter 3

End of the Honeymoon

The bowling ball is heavier than I can handle, and I try another. At last, I find one I can manage. I glance over my shoulder at Seth and Rhoda, who already have their dorky bowling shoes on, and hurry to join them. The pulsing music doesn't drown out the clunk of balls, the clatter of pins, and the shouts of joy or dismay among the other players. The aroma of nachos and burgers drifts from the snack bar.

"Let me give you a few pointers," he says. Seth's personal red marble-looking ball slides from his hand and plows down the pins at the end of the lane. He smirks. Rhoda claps. I squint, my hand going slick.

"Don't cross this line." He gestures to the tape across the near end of the lane. "Just aim and send the ball down there. Nothing to it."

I swallow. It's not that I've never bowled before, but never with them. I don't want them to think badly of me. The deceptively light ball I'd selected gets heavier as I move across the wood parquet floor, shined to a high luster and surely reflecting my terrified expression. I take a deep breath, step forward a few paces, swing the ball, and let go.

The thud it makes when it hits the floor makes me wince. I look around and see indulgent expressions on the bowlers to my right and left. Then, in tandem, they both move to the line, gracefully let their bowling balls slide, and knock down every pin in their respective lanes before my wobbling ball teeters off into the left gutter. My cheeks burn, and I turn to go sit down in shame.

Rhoda tells me to watch her closely, and she moves with confidence to the lane. She leaves one pin to the left and the right, and then knocks them down with a second throw. Sweat breaks out across the back of my neck.

We continue to bowl, not even keeping score while Seth and Rhoda give tips to help me improve. Over the next half hour, I do improve. I begin to relax and enjoy the game.

We play three more games and keep score. My scores rise each time until I actually win the final game. I am elated. I'd not been enthusiastic when Seth and Rhoda had suggested an afternoon of bowling, but I'm already looking forward to the next time.

We change our shoes, turn in our equipment, and head for the parking lot. Seth is quiet. I am jubilant. I rein in my excitement. Were I with anyone else, I'd be crowing, "That was so much fun! I plastered you in that last one."

As if hearing my thoughts, Rhoda ducks her head. Seth walks with a stiff gait at my side. His frown is thunderous, and his eyes are hard. A small flutter of concern wiggles in my stomach.

We reach the car. Seth gazes off into the distance, his mouth an upside-down horseshoe of discontent. He starts the car, and the silence is oppressive. We drive for ten minutes, mute and tense.

Suddenly, his hand flashes out and crashes into the windshield. I jump, surprised not to see spider cracks crawl across the glass surface.

His eyes bore into mine, angry, smoldering. "You stole my abilities in the spirit realm, and you have the nerve to be pleased about it?" His voice lashes me.

"Seth, it was just a ga—"

"Never, ever say the spirit realm is a game!" His growl goes down my spine and punches my heart. He's shaking with fury.

The lump in my belly is huge. I wonder if it has three finger holes.

* * *

"Pick us up," his silky voice had said over the phone. "We're going out tonight."

Please, please, not bowling. I hear the words over and over in my mind as I drive to their house. He and Rhoda are more dressed up than usual, and I relax. They'd never bowl in those clothes.

We drive for an hour. The Delaware state line flashes by before we turn into the kind of area I haven't visited for many months. My life has changed so much since I got involved in the Ministry. I feel smug to realize it. The bottom drops out when we pull over, and Seth leads the way toward the neon lights and loud music of a seedy neighborhood bar.

Stale beer assaults my nose as we enter, and the low cloud of cigarette smoke is almost opaque. Seth and Rhoda look comfortable here, which surprises me. They take a table in a corner, and he orders each of us drinks. I'm dumbfounded. Is this a test of some kind?

I keep waiting for Seth to say something to put this outing in perspective. Instead, he drinks, we drink, he orders more. I pay with my credit card. Of course. The conversation is light and meaningless. I laugh at his jokes and sway to the music from the juke box.

At last Seth pushes his drink away and captures my eyes with his piercing blue ones. "Do you feel better now?" he asks.

I frown and take my hand off my cool glass. "What do you mean?"

"We're here because of you. Do you feel better now that you've manifested what is in you by drinking and losing control?"

My head is buzzing from the unaccustomed impact of alcohol, and the music seems to get louder every moment. His eyes won't let go of mine. "You said to come here. I didn't ask to."

"Your spirit was asking. Your dirty, selfish, lustful, drunken spirit was crying out all week for this release. God told me to go ahead and let you manifest it by bringing you here. Answer my question."

It takes me a beat or two to even remember the question. "I didn't want to come here," is all I can come up with.

He scratches his short beard and shakes his head slowly. "You're mad at me." Everything seems to be moving at less than normal speed to me. His words elongate and become harder for me to comprehend. "You're mad because I put you through this, and tomorrow you're going to pay for it with a big headache and a sick stomach. But even more, you're mad at God for it, since He's the One who told me to let you do this."

"I'm not mad. I'm confused. You said to come here; you said to drink these drinks. You sat here and drank with us."

A buzz is hounding my head and making it difficult to focus.

"As I said, this is you—the real you—showing itself. How do you like it?"

Tears further fog my vision. I want to leave but am not sure my legs will support me. What does he want from me?

His deep sigh tells me he is disappointed in my lack of response. He slides out of the booth, motions to Rhoda and me, and we follow him out. The cooler night air helps to revive me somewhat, and I'm glad of it. I shake my head. Seth takes the keys, and we get in the car for the drive home. I can't wait to get to bed and forget this confusing evening.

The landscape outside is black as we cross Amish country with its lack of electric lights. I am in a daze and unsure of where we are.

His voice hisses. "I want you to manifest the demons that are in you. Now!"

He's talked about this many times, how people's demons often are evidenced by what they say and the voice they are said in. I've never had an experience like that and don't know what to do.

"Manifest how much you hate me!" he shouts.

I jump in my seat and then work up a movie-type voice out of desperation. "I hate you! I hate you, I hate you!" I croak.

His slap comes from nowhere and penetrates much deeper than the skin of my arm where it lands. His eyes scorch me. "That's not manifesting. You do what you're told. You manifest your demons!"

I try again and am hit again. And again. And again.

"I don't know what you want!" I hold my arm and my side where he's been striking me to protect myself. "Maybe I don't have any demons, if none want to come out."

"Oh, you have them. You're infested with them. And tonight they caused all three of us to have to go to that bar and drink to make them happy." He begins to punch me in earnest.

I lurch against my seat belt as he slams on the brakes. The car skids but stays in the lane. I smell melted rubber and asphalt as we rock to a stop.

I sob and reach for the door handle, scrabbling to find it in the darkness. He bolts from the car, rounds the hood, and grabs me. I tumble out of the car. As he continues to punch and slap me, I hit the shoulder and land in a heap, begging him to stop. He shoves me into the ditch and glares at me.

Before I have time to process what is happening, he circles the car and gets in. The car jumps forward, my door slams shut, and I am left in a spray of pebbles as they drive away.

The alcohol prevents me from getting up. I curl up in the ditch, weeping. Two red taillights dwindle in the darkness, then go over a hill and disappear. I wail with disbelief and fear.

I have no purse, no cell phone, no idea where I am. The cold air wraps around me and forms an icy barrier that holds me in the ditch darkness, helpless. My eyes strain to see lights, my ears ache for the sound of an engine. The night closes in.

* * *

Tears rain down my cold cheeks. I try to find a tissue in a pocket and come up empty. I sniffle as deeply as I can to keep from making a mess on my face and rub my sleeve over my eyes. Paralysis attacks my brain, as well as my limbs. No light is visible in any direction. The bowl of the sky is studded with stars as remote and unhelpful as the taillights of the car that vanished several minutes before.

When the drone of an engine penetrates my soggy mind, I raise my head. It pulls to a stop in front of me and the door opens, beckoning me back into the warm embrace of familiarity. Seth glowers from the driver's seat.

I scramble inside and slam the door, locking it to be sure he can't push me out.

"You're worthless, you know that?"

I shiver, not caring what he says. I'm safe again.

"The least you could have done was get up and start walking to a phone somewhere. But here I come back and find you in the same ditch you were in when I left." His hands tighten on the wheel, and he puts his foot to the gas.

I let out a tiny sigh of relief. I doubt he'll try to push me out while we're moving. I hope he won't.

"You have no idea what's really inside you, how much God hates you, how ugly you are to everyone around you. Do you realize that if you'd sat in that ditch all night and frozen to death, you would have gone to hell? How can you stand yourself? You're almost beyond redemption, almost beyond our efforts."

I hear only one word in his tirade. *Almost.*

I cling to it and vow to do better.

* * *

Twisting in the wind

AS ASHAMED AS I AM TO LOOK BACK and see how easily my whole life was turned upside down by Seth, I can also see the pattern of what took place more clearly in retrospect. Living alone for the first year in the group, I had no contact even with my mother. When I was allowed to see her at Christmas time, she was brought to the house where I was living-blindfolded. My sole contacts each day were Seth and Rhoda.

To someone hungry for affection, acceptance and affirmation, having that much concentrated attention from two people I thought were godly and very spiritual was intoxicating. Phone calls, going out together, watching movies together. It seemed I was never alone without hope of them getting in touch soon. My world revolved around what Seth was teaching me and trying to show them both I'd learned my lessons well.

I had only started my journey back to God when I got involved with Seth and Rhoda. To say I was biblically ignorant is to understate the case. I was a blank page. Seth picked up his pen and began to write all over me. I didn't realize until much later that he twisted

Scriptures like corkscrews, taking verses out of context and reworking my mental processes to reflect his views.

■ To say I was biblically ignorant is to understate the case. I was a blank page. ■

In coming to grips with how easily I was duped, I've struggled to read the Bible. When I come across verses Seth liked to quote, I feel physically ill sometimes. The blessing of God is that when I take a breath, pray for strength, and then read the passage in its proper context, I can usually see it meant the opposite (or at least something completely different) from what I was taught. It's a slow, painful process that anyone who has been misled by a Bible-quoting cult must undergo.

Seth spent a lot of time in the Old Testament whenever he was quoting. This seems to be a common occurrence with deliverance-centered teaching. In the Old Testament, God lets His anger out on the page as the nation of Israel (or specific individuals) turn away from Him time after time. When read as a complete passage, the meaning of these verses is clear. However, to someone lifting them from the page for his own purposes, they can be used to wound, confuse, and batter.

The Psalms and prophetic books have many passages of raw anguish and anger. Seth would turn them against me, telling me this was what God thought of me and others—everyone, it seemed, except him. I was to remember who and what I was, and see how incredibly disgusted with me God must be.

"For I acknowledge my transgressions, and my sin is always before me. Against You, You only, have I sinned, and done this evil in Your sight—that You may be found just when You speak, and blameless when You judge. Behold, I was brought forth in iniquity, and in sin my mother conceived me. (Psalm 51:3-7, NKJV)

"For I am ready to fall, and my sorrow is continually before me. For I will declare my iniquity; I will be in anguish over my sin." (Psalm 38:17-18, NKJV)

"For the lips of an immoral woman drip honey, and her mouth is smoother than oil; but in the end she is bitter as wormwood, sharp as a two-edged sword. Her feet go down to death, her steps lay hold of hell. Lest you ponder her path of life—her ways are unstable." (Proverbs 5:3-6, NKJV)

He liked to call group members by names from the Bible and then said the verses that contained those names were written for us. Babylon, Cain, Jezebel, Esau, and Pharisee all became epithets with verses of condemnation right there in black and white to drive us to believe God had no real use for any of us. He specifically called my sister and me Oholah and Oholibah, the names used in the Bible for "sister" harlots. This meant all verses related to harlotry were fair game to sling at us and with which to berate us. Now that I can study the Bible myself, it is abundantly clear these names and condemnations were not meant for anybody. Ezekiel 23:4 says, "Samaria is Oholah, and Jerusalem is Oholibah" (NKJV). But we were forbidden to read passages beyond what he told us to read.

By the end of my time in the cult, that list of acceptable things had shrunk to the "red text" of Jesus' words, the book of John, and the book of 1 John. Each was twisted so that it brought condemnation, not relief.

No matter what I did, it would never be good enough. No matter how I tried, everything was tainted with my sin. After a while, my bruised spirit couldn't even lift itself up to try to reach God. I could only do what Seth said to do—pray the prayers he taught and focus on trying to keep as many demons away from myself as possible. My only hope of salvation was to do as Seth said, since God liked him. God's only way to love us was to give us Seth to correct and direct us. His unending message was, "Repent or perish." He found a great deal of fodder for his berating by quoting only what he wanted us to hear.

When your head is clear, you can look at a person and say, "He's not walking the talk." You can then discount what the person says. But when your whole life centers around one person who speaks with great authority and holds your whole spiritual future in his hands, it's hard to be so discerning. A good deceiver knows what he's doing, and has a ready answer for any discrepancies. When Seth talked to me, the answer was simple: It was all my fault.

"I am the greatest of all sinners," he'd say, "but God doesn't hold it against me because I'm only acting out what is inside of you. Your sin is so great, your impurity so overwhelming, that it manifests itself through me toward you. If you were better, I'd be better. I take this on as a holy burden on your behalf, but it's a heavy one."

■ When Seth talked to me, the answer was simple: It was all my fault. ■

By this logic, he could swear, be physically abusive, demand that I take him to a motel and have sex with him, or even command me to hit my mother to discipline her—all of which are clearly sin—but not be held accountable for any of it. He said he hated doing it, but he was trying to save our souls. If we didn't listen to what he said and do what he told us to do, we would be breaking faith with what God had put into our lives and we would be assured of going to hell. Not only that, we'd take everyone with whom we had contact along with us. God hated us. Our only chance was to come to repentance before He returns. The group around Seth was a specially chosen ministry, established by God. If we walked away from so great a calling, there was no chance for us.

Just as negative verses were twisted and morphed into rods of punishment, positive verses of affirmation were clearly about and for Seth (and sometimes Rhoda). He was brutal, sarcastic, controlling, narcissistic, and unpredictable. Gentle one moment, physically abusive the next, he was still able to draw me to believe what he said by playing off the various sides of his personality. I received just enough positive strokes to keep me striving to live up to what he wanted.

Bible verses that described the role of a prophet or that attributed positive characteristics to a believer were about Seth. He and Rhoda firmly believe they are the "two witnesses" described in the book of Revelation who will convict the world of sin in the end times. Because these witnesses are described as being impervious to being hurt, they said their bodies would be changed into something wonderful when this ministry begins. If we were diligent and upheld the part of the ministry entrusted to us, we might hope for something similar.

Though encouraging at the beginning, Seth's teachings settled into a pattern that led straight to self-doubt, humiliation, and fear. I was probably going to hell; I should be put out of the ministry to keep it pure; God hated me; God wished I'd never been born; He was sorry He'd made the human race, and me in particular; I was demon spawn. Clearly, I was not doing my best to take control of spirits and bind them. They were still able to get to Seth and make him have to manifest what was actually going on inside of me.

If I tried to refute what Seth said, he reminded me that the Bible said we should be "casting down arguments and every high thing that exalts itself against the knowledge of God, bringing every thought into captivity to the obedience of Christ" (2 Corinthians 10:5, NKJV). In the world of the cult, obedience to Christ meant obedience to Seth.

People who twist Scripture to ensnare other people are smart enough to include bits of truth in the mix of deception. Since he quoted verses from the Bible, it was hard for me to dispute what Seth said. It was right there on the page. To fight him was to fight God and His Word. That was clearly a losing game from any angle.

■ Since he quoted verses from the Bible, It was hard for me to dispute what Seth said. ■

Much of my recovery from the cult has involved re-examining each point of the so-called theology Seth drilled into me, comparing it with the Bible and listening to the counsel of truly godly people who have studied deeply. Rather than replacing one "authority" with another when I turned to those who wanted to help me recover, I began to learn how to study and discern for myself. I've moved from complete bondage to Seth's words and come to live in the breathtaking freedom of the truth.

I am free in Christ, washed by His blood, cleansed by His sacrifice, safe in His hands, with all eternity to explore my relationship with Him and worship at His feet.

If you have come through a time of spiritual deception, it is entirely possible you are confused about your salvation. Perhaps you have picked up this book because you're curious about cults and have no assurance that you belong to God and will spend eternity with Him in heaven. In either case, you don't have to spend another minute in that state.

You might find sample prayers in other books or pamphlets, but I'm not going to give you one. Talk to God in your own words. Tell Him you know you are a sinner and have gone against His perfect will for your life. Be specific about ways you've wandered. Then accept by faith His payment for every one of those sins—and those you've not yet even committed—by Jesus' death on the cross on your behalf. Ask Him to fill you with His Holy Spirit, and the peaceful assurance of His love.

Live in the light of His truth, not the darkness of confusion any more.

"As you therefore have received Christ Jesus the Lord, so walk in Him, rooted and built up in Him and established in the faith, as you have been taught, abounding in it with thanksgiving. Beware lest anyone cheat you through philosophy and empty deceit, according to the tradition of men, according to the basic principles of the world, and not according to Christ." (Colossians 2:6-8, NKJV)

What I was told…	**The truth**
God hates and despise me.	"Greater love has no one than this, than to and despises lay down one's life for his friends." (John15:13) "But God demonstrates His own love toward us, in that while we were still sinners, Christ died for us." (Rom. 5:8) "For the Father Himself loves you, because you have loved Me [Christ], and have believed that I came forth from God." (John 16:27)
I am probably bound for a hell, after a life of complete degeneracy, apart from God.	"But as it is written, 'Eye has not seen, nor ear heard, nor have entered into the heart of man the things which God has prepared for those who love Him." (1 Cor. 2:9) "I have been crucified with Christ: it is no longer I who live, but Christ lives in me; and the life which I now live in the flesh I live by faith in the Son of God, who loved me and gave Himself for me." (Gal. 2:20) "Most assuredly, I say to you, he who hears My word and believes in Him who sent Me has everlasting life, and shall not come into judgment, but has passed from death into life." (John 5:24)

Demons have the ability to invade me, control me, and keep me from being what God wants me to be.	"Who is he who condemns? It is Christ who died, and furthermore is also risen, who is even at the right hand of God, who also makes intercession for us. Who shall separate us from the love of Christ? Shall tribulation, or distress, or persecution, or famine, or nakedness, or peril, or sword?… For I am persuaded that neither death nor life, nor angels nor principalities nor powers, nor things present nor things to come, or height nor depth, nor any other created thing, shall be able to separate us from the love of God which is in Christ Jesus our Lord." (Rom. 8:34-35, 38-39)
I am filthy And unforgivable.	"There is therefore now no condemnation to those who are in Christ Jesus, who do not walk according to the flesh, but according to the Spirit." (Rom. 8:1)
Seth and his "ministry" were my only hope for life." Eventual redemption.	"For God so loved the world that He gave His "ministry" only begotten Son, that whoever believes in were my Him should not perish but have everlasting only hope for life." (John 3:16) "And this is the testimony: that God has given us eternal life, and this life is in His Son. He who has the Son has life; he who does not have the Son of God does not have life. These things I have written to you who believe in the name of the Son of God, that you may know that you have eternal life, and that you may continue to believe in the name of the Son of God." (1 John 5:11-13)

■ Thinking It Through…■

How to Wash a Brain

Most people would view the process Jennifer went through as brainwashing. A more accurate term is mind control. Cult expert Steven Hassan distinguishes between the two by the overt signs they display.

> "Brainwashing is typically coercive. The person knows at the outset that he is in the hands of an enemy. Abusive treatment, even torture, is usually involved." He goes on to contrast: "Mind control, also called 'thought reform,' is more subtle and sophisticated. Its perpetrators are regarded as friends or peers, so the person is much less defensive. He unwittingly participates by cooperating with his controllers and giving them private information that he does not know will be used against him. The new belief system is internalized into a new identity structure."[2]

Lists have been compiled that seek to define the steps of mind control. Though they vary in length and complexity, each of these systems includes the idea of breaking down a person's previous concepts and self-identity, building up a new set of ideas and personality, and reinforcing the "revised person" through promises, threats, and other means. Edgar Schein labeled the steps as unfreezing, changing, and refreezing.[3]

Perhaps the most comprehensive description of the steps in mind control comes from Robert J. Lifton.[4] He lists eight, most of which Jennifer experienced:

Milieu Control. Everything around the new recruit is controlled—who she sees, where she goes, what she does, sources of information. For Jennifer, this took the form of Seth weeding out her books and music until he was satisfied with what she had (almost nothing); keeping her at home alone for a year after joining the group with access only to him and Rhoda for companionship and training; no contact with friends and family, even though some members of her family were in the group already.

Mystical Manipulation. Also called "planned spontaneity," this involves controlling and planning everything that happens to the recruit, but making it look like it is God-orchestrated. When Seth would call Jennifer in the middle of the night to ask if she was all right, saying he'd been awakened by God and was worried about her, it felt like he was standing between God and her as a direct conduit of concern.

Demand for Purity. A strict line is drawn between pure and impure, good and evil, whether in the world or inside the recruit. The obvious goal is to rid oneself and one's environment of evil and only be left with good. By continually adding new items to the list of good and evil, this can become a moving target. The prayers Jennifer was instructed to pray continually to keep "demons" out of herself, her home, and her life were designed to conform her to the cult's way of thinking and make her feel she was contributing to the work of the ministry. In fact, they only left her exhausted and paranoid.

Cult of Confession. We often hear that confession is good for the soul. A manipulative cult leader takes this adage to the extreme, with regular sessions in which the recruit is first criticized, then required to criticize herself, all with the goal of self-improvement. In Seth's case, he not only told Jennifer how he viewed her and used Scripture he'd twisted to say how God felt about her, he also demanded that she "manifest the demons" inside herself. This meant she should sound like a demon, thrash about like a possessed person, and release the evil inside her. Since she never could figure out what he wanted in these sessions, she would fall into the trap of trying to make up things and put on voices. This only enraged him and led to physical abuse. The outcome was that Jennifer felt she was truly not in touch with God since she couldn't even figure out what was wrong with her, much less get it out.

Sacred Science. Many cults blend in bits of scientific knowledge to give their own dogma an official seal of approval, or associate themselves with the names of experts in different fields to try to lend credibility. By combining spiritual principles with psychological terms and information, for instance, it can take the science to a spiritual level and also elevate the spiritual to a scientific fact.

Loading of the Language. We all hate it when people say things we don't understand. With cults, the words themselves may have several layers of meaning. A word or phrase can be stripped down to a new and literal meaning only understood within the group. This gives insiders a feeling of smug knowledge as they use phrases and words that are spiritual shorthand for what is viewed as much deeper concepts. In fact, the people using the phrases have ceased to think, rather than thinking deeply. When Seth had trained Jennifer to view herself negatively by citing Bible verses that implied she was unclean and destined for hell, all he had to say was, "Woe to you!" or "Brood of vipers!" and it immediately triggered an entire subtext of meaning that struck her to the soul.

Doctrine over Person. When it comes to spiritual knowledge, most people acknowledge they will never completely understand everything. (For instance, try to define and communicate the Trinity.) There is a built-in expectation that some things have to be believed, without being understood. Often, believing it will seem counterintuitive. Cults capitalize on this feeling by encouraging recruits to put themselves aside and prefer the "truth" over their conflicting feelings and experience of it. This helps shut down critical thinking. Jennifer was told demons infested just about everything, and that she herself was riddled with them. Since she could not "manifest" them to please Seth, she had only his word to go on as to her condition. In putting aside her own doubts and accepting his "greater" understanding, she chose to buy into the doctrine at her own peril.

Dispensing of Existence. Just as firm lines are drawn between good and evil, so are they drawn between those who have the truth and those "outside." Non-group members are necessarily of far less importance than those in the cult. This works to raise the ego of the recruit as she is taught "greater" truths, and also serves as a terrifying threat should she try to leave the group. To do so would be to go into that non-existing, non-important, utterly clueless part of humanity destined for hell. Jennifer felt the flames of hell were always hovering just out of sight, waiting for her to slip and be consumed. No teaching of God's love, Christ's sacrifice for her sins, eternal security, or resting in faith were presented or encouraged. The threat of separation from family members in the group was also profoundly frightening.

Does every cult leader consciously take his or her followers down this tortuous path of self-deception and indoctrination? Some do. For others, it is a roster of tactics that have worked in the past. The reward for the cult leader is obedient, revering followers and the ego boost this brings. Eventually, he may begin to believe his own press-making him all the more dangerous.

Mind control is subtle. It wouldn't work if it were blatant, as shown by brainwashing techniques used in China many years ago. Once the prisoner was released from the environment of the brainwashing, he generally could go back to rational thought. For mind control to be effective, it must work even when the controller (the cult leader or a deputy) is not around. Jennifer spent a lot of time alone, but still stuck to what she was told to do because she'd been led to believe it was necessary work for the benefit of the world and her own soul.

We all hunger for that kind of validation. We are all ripe for indoctrination if we're not observant and defensive.

Resources

Please visit our website: www.JenniferRedcay.com for any additional lists of resources we compile. Those listed below will get you started.

Cults: What Parents Should Know, The American Family Foundation, Joan Carol Ross and Michael D. Langone, A Lyle Stewart Book, 1988.

By Hook or By Crook: How Cults Lure Christians, Harold Bussell, McCracken Press, 1993.

*Cults In Our Midst: The Continuing Fight Against their Hidden Menace,
Margaret Thaler Singer, Jossey-Bass Books, 2003. Combatting Cult
Mind Control, Steven Hassan, Park Street Press, 1988, 1990.
Twisted Scriptures: Breaking Free from Churches that Abuse, Mary Alice
Chrnalogar, Zondervan, 1998, 2000.*

Chapter 4

The Day I Died

Thump. Thump. Thump.

Thumpity-thumpity-thumpity.

There are two of us. We are entwined. We breathe the same air, share the same blood. I can almost hear your thoughts. My heart beats, and yours echoes in a thrilling staccato.

Thump. Thump. Thump.

Thumpity-thumpity-thumpity.

I want to hold you inside me and keep you safe from everything in the world. My body is your blanket, your shell, your haven.

I have never longed for anything as much as being a mother. Your mother. To feel you grow and kick and turn inside me. To push you into the world with effort and pain and great joy, and look on your sweet face for the first time—knowing my heart is forever no longer my own.

I feel you shiver inside me and wonder if you know...

"Is she ready yet? It's almost lunch time. Let's get moving."

"She's ready."

No! I'm not ready! I'll never be ready! Please, please, please—

Thump-thump. Thump-thump. Thump-thump-thump.

Thumpity-thumpity-thumpity-thumpity-thumpity.

You feel my fear. You taste my sorrow. You shudder as I do when he touches my body and invades your space.

I cry out for both of us. My tears would fill the Dead Sea. My heart is bursting.

Thumpity-thumpity-thumpity-thumpity-thum—

Thump-thump-thump. Thump-thump-thump.
The roar of the vacuum is overshadowed by the silence echoing within.
Thump…thump…thump…
I am torn in two.

* * *

Puppet on a string

DESPITE MY INITIAL DISLIKE, it would have been almost inconceivable that I not be drawn to Seth. The cult never included more than about ten people—three of them male: Seth, a man he married my sister to in California, and a teen boy. Other than when I worked as a waitress at a diner, I had no contact with other people. I kept my head down at work and did my job, always afraid demons would jump from other people onto me. Though a friendly waitress earns better tips, I couldn't take the risk. Seth was the only male constant in my life.

From the beginning, he told all the women in the group that they had sexual fantasies about him, and they'd need to control them. To an outsider, this would be preposterous. Tall, skinny, with a scraggly beard, Seth held no physical attraction other than his magnetic blue eyes. However, much like someone left on an isolated island with only one other person, over time he became my universe, and I grew to wish I meant more to him than merely a group member.

A master manipulator, Seth fed on my dependence and turned my own desires back against me, leading me just far enough along to keep me bound to him. Rhoda, his wife, was many years older and very heavy set. He did not seem interested in her in any physical way—a recipe for disaster.

■ **Over time he became my universe.** ■

When I first met Seth he had "prophesied" over me, saying my husband would be a great man of God and do mighty things for the

Lord. The fact that he'd told me to let my husband leave me, and so I no longer had a husband, did not dampen my desire to see that so-called prophecy come true. I simply transferred my attention to Seth and began to fantasize what would happen if somehow Rhoda were not in the picture. He helped the situation along by hinting she might die if she didn't step up to the plate and do what she was supposed to do. At the time I assumed he meant God might strike her down. Now, I'm not so sure.

Several years after I joined the cult, Seth began to make advances. Each time he made it clear it was not him coming on to me, but rather that my personal desires were so strong they were forcing him to manifest them toward me. Steeped in the twisted theology of demons in everything, used to accepting what he said as truth, it didn't make much of a ripple in my mind. It should have, but whatever happened was my fault, in his opinion, even though he instigated and ordered everything. It was a slick way to avoid any responsibility for his actions.

Eventually our encounters escalated from heavy petting to full sexual intimacy. Seth would wait until Rhoda went to work on the night shift, then call and tell me to pick him up. He would direct me to drive to another county, where I'd rent a motel room. Sometimes I would come home from work to find garments in my room laid out for use that night. A raincoat. A negligee. Something provocative and not at all to my taste. I was to wear this and nothing else when I picked him up.

I craved closeness to another human being who loved me. Cut off from normal society, I was starved for affection—even that which ended in roughness and abuse. After our "sessions," sometimes Seth would jerk and seem to have a fit. He said he was fighting the devil for me on God's behalf by letting out my demons of lust. I am now certain demons were involved, but not in the way he described his role.

■ Cut off from normal society, I was starved for affection. ■

After each sexual encounter, he demanded I get rid of everything I'd had with me at the time. My clothes. My contact lenses. Even my driver's license, since I'd used it to rent the room. One time I had to get rid of my car because we'd used it instead of a room. The car I bought to replace it turned out to be a real lemon and served as a vicious reminder of what we'd done.

Seth delighted in degrading me. He also enjoyed humiliating both me and Rhoda and once found an exquisite method to do so: I had to confess to her everything that happened on one of our "dates." Seth insisted I lie about my responses to him, to exaggerate them, and to tell Rhoda every graphic detail of our sexual encounter. This embarrassed both of us. I confessed; she forgave. If either of us didn't do our job, he would have Scripture ready to berate us.

In the Bible, Christians are told to confess their sins to God, and He is faithful and righteous to forgive. This contrived confession went to his wife, not God, and was intended as anything but cleansing. Though she said she forgave me, I cannot imagine how hurt and enraged she must have been. The whole point of biblical confession is to clear the air between the believer and God, and then the believer tries not to repeat the sin again. No effort was made to stop the cycle.

Seth loved to quote from the Old Testament. Because of his obsession with Old Testament law, he demanded I notify him whenever I started my period, since I would be "unclean" for that week, and then not contact him until I'd finished. I would leave a message on his answering machine. Initially, these times of solitude were painful for me. But over time I grew to look forward to them. No contact meant no berating, no beatings, no attention. I could catch up on my sleep. I could relax a little. My menstrual cycles kept me sane.

I was regular as clockwork, so I knew almost immediately when I became pregnant. Labor Day weekend, 2005—how ironic. As Hurricane Katrina roared into New Orleans, a storm of pain and agony raged into my life, as well. I felt just as helpless as the people along the Gulf.

"I think I'm pregnant," I told him.

He snorted. "That's not possible. I'm doing God's work, and He will protect me from that."

I shook my head. "I'm sick every morning, I've skipped my period, and there are other signs—"

■ "I think I'm pregnant," I told him. ■

"I'm telling you, it's not possible. You think you know everything, but we both know you are frequently wrong." He looked away, already interested in something else. "But if it makes you feel better, get one of those home pregnancy tests. Then you'll see I'm right, as usual. Call Rhoda and give her the results."

I could not think of anything I wanted to do less. "And then what?"

"Take care of it."

Wanting to be sure I understood, I said, "You're telling me to get the test, and then if it's positive, you want me to get an abortion. Is that what you're saying?" My heart hammered, and my stomach lurched.

"Yes. Don't contact me until you're clean again."

My mind reeled with the thought of losing the one thing I longed for with all my heart—a child. Despite the circumstances, I already loved this baby. It wasn't the baby's fault that I was in an impossible situation. He or she should not have to pay for my mistakes. There had to be another way.

As though reading what I was thinking, Seth slammed the door on any hope. "Don't even think about trying to leave and have this baby on your own," he hissed. "You couldn't do anything more selfish than that! Anyone you come in contact with will be dragged straight to hell with you. I will hunt you down and find you and kill you both. Do you understand?"

My baby in hell. My baby in hell! I could not tolerate the idea. How could I condemn an innocent to a life on the run with me, and leave a trail of devastation and damnation in our wake?

I bought the test. It showed positive. I called Rhoda and gave her the news. It felt like I'd put an enormous roller coaster in motion with no brakes or seatbelts.

* * *

Rhoda rode with me in the car to the clinic in Baltimore. Of all the people in the world to have with me at such a heart-wrenching time, she was at the bottom of my list. Her stern face was eloquent with disapproval and anger. As we drove, she said Seth had instructed her to "manifest our demons" regarding this situation to each other and get them all out.

At last she had her opportunity to tell me how much she hated me, was jealous of me, wanted me dead. It added another layer of injury to my numb, battered heart.

We arrived at the clinic. Outside, it resembled an apartment building. Inside, a hallway, lined with women waiting for the door to open, led to the office. Some looked around in a way that told me they'd been there before. Others bore holes in the carpet with their empty stares. No one spoke.

A clerk gave me paperwork to complete, including a frightening list of possible complications. Rhoda sat with me as I filled it out, and then she prayed with me to bind the demons of each complication to ward it off. I paid the money and waited.

Abortion clinics charge different rates for various services. The most expensive procedure includes plenty of pain medication. I didn't have money for that, so I went with the cheaper version. I put it on my credit card, just like all the other things Seth and Rhoda made me pay for. He'd offered to pay some of the fee, but I felt so horrible I refused to allow him to give me money to kill my child. I wrapped my arms around my middle and wished I could turn to stone.

Once a nurse called me back to the room where the abortion would be performed, the process became like a revolving door. Women were wheeled in and out of rooms, from one place to another, finally ending up in the recovery room. I will not describe the abortion. There are plenty of books and articles you can read for a realistic look at this horrible act. It was painful beyond belief, and violent. I came out of the operating room physically alive but emotionally as dead as my baby. I cried and cried.

In the recovery room, a young girl's mother stood beside her bed. Their cell phone rang, and the mother passed it to her daughter. It became obvious from the conversation that she was talking to her baby's father.

Suddenly her voice rose in hysteria. "Don't tell me that! Don't say it! It's too late—I've already done it! Oh, don't say that!" she wailed with the broken heart of missed opportunity and betrayal.

After time spent in recovery, we were discharged. A nurse told Rhoda to get me something to eat on the way home. I broke down again in the car as Rhoda drove.

"Why are you crying? It's over now," she snapped.

"I killed my baby," I sobbed.

She stopped to get me a hamburger. I couldn't gag much of it down. The world around me shrank to a dark, dank tunnel, and I knew I would never find the end. If I could have gotten out of the car and lay down in a ditch to die, I would have done so.

■ The world around me shrank
to a dark, dank tunnel. ■

I cried myself to sleep that night. I went to work and then came home on my break. I remember sobbing and sobbing on my bathroom floor. In my distress, I ripped my shirt in half. I didn't know what else to do.

When Seth called, he heard the tears in my voice and rebuked me. He showed no sympathy or concern about my painful experience and told me I deserved the punishment. I had to pull myself together in order to survive, so I stuffed it all deep down inside.

I bled for nearly ten days after the abortion, a terrible reminder of what a horrible thing I'd done. Most awful, however, even though my mother and I lived in the same house at this point, Seth forbid me to tell her what had happened. I could not turn to her for comfort, or even chastisement (which I felt I richly deserved). I bottled up my feelings and tried to put one foot in front of the other to keep going. I don't remember that time very clearly. It was the darkest season of my life.

* * *

Despite a prohibition on sexual activity for several weeks following the abortion, Seth expected me to pick right back up where we'd left off, as though a human being had not been sacrificed for our sin. But it wasn't long before he lost interest in me sexually and turned his focus to physical abuse and beatings. He told me God wanted to punish me for what I'd done, so I must gain fifty pounds immediately.

I'd lost some weight in the cult, then put on about fifteen pounds with the pregnancy. Adding another fifty meant my double shifts as a waitress would be agony on my feet. I had to eat junk food and drink milk at night, and when I didn't gain the weight fast enough, he beat me. If I complained, he beat me. Seth made it clear the punishment he administered came from God, and He truly hated me inside and out.

Being significantly overweight made me miserable. We moved into a new house that apparently had mold problems, and I developed asthma symptoms. My heart became black and empty, and I had no one to turn to for comfort because Seth had forbidden me to talk to my mother and God wasn't listening.

* * *

After we left the cult, I received counseling regarding the abortion. It saved my sanity and helped on my march back to spiritual and mental health. Women who go through a terminated pregnancy, especially at the instigation of people around them, live with guilt and shame that has no outlet. Post-abortion counseling is imperative to restore a woman's emotions, mental health, and relationship with God.

God blessed me with a fabulous counselor. Carol has never had an abortion herself, but she has a true heart for those who have been through the wrenching experience of terminating the life of a child—for whatever reason. Her warmth and understanding brought the first rays back to my lightless heart. Many women find hope and strength by going through counseling in a group setting. Carol usually takes her groups through a ten-week Bible study. However, since I had to deal not only with the aftermath of the abortion but also the struggle with cult-related issues, she decided we would do the study one-on-one.

At our first session, I received a notebook to put papers into each week as we progressed, and two books: *Her Choice to Heal,* by Synda Masse and Joan Phillips, and *H.E.A.R.T. Manual: Healing the Effects of Abortion Related Trauma,* by Heartbeat International. Each week I read a chapter from the book and did the homework, which included looking up Scriptures about who I am in Christ, forgiveness, fear, anger, and other related topics. This rejuvenated me.

At a typical session, Carol would play a praise song to set the mood, and she'd sing along. Initially my insecurity kept me from singing and I would just mouth the words if I knew them. As we progressed, however, I began to sing and worship the Lord for bringing me out of my shame. Every session opened and closed with prayer.

Early in the counseling process, we went over the symptoms of post-abortion syndrome. I certainly fit the profile. We discussed my anger, fear, and shame. Then we focused on God's heart toward me and what I did. As we studied the character of God, I drew strength from His unchangeable nature and bottomless forgiveness.

To help me gauge my progress, Carol asked me to draw a picture of how I felt inside. I drew a big, black hole. At the end of the ten weeks, we repeated this exercise. Though I still drew a black hole, it had shrunk to be almost invisible.

■ As we studied the character of God, I drew strength from His unchangeable nature and bottomless forgiveness. ■

The session when we worked on forgiveness became incredibly important. I blamed a lot of people for the abortion: my aunt for introducing me to Seth, my mother, my ex-husband for not fighting for me when I got sucked into the cult, the doctor and nurse involved in the procedure, Seth, Rhoda, myself. The longer the list grew, the more I realized I was steeped in anger and bitterness. Letting it go made me feel light enough to float. It was a tremendous milestone. Tears washed every session, but they were healing, cleansing, beneficial. They began to wash away the dead tissue muffling my heart and blocking my ability to experience emotions—good or bad.

As a closing to our time of healing and processing, I held a memorial for my baby, to recognize her as a person, and to let go of the guilt, shame, and pain once and for all. We held it at the home of my spiritual counselors, and I invited Carol and a small group of family members. Prior to the service, Carol suggested I name the baby. I stressed over it for days, fearful of giving her the wrong name. But as I prayed for her and for continued healing, the name flowed into my heart.

At the memorial, Carol played a special song that captured the viewpoint of a little boy going to meet his mother and asking the Lord why he'd never met her before. The Lord replied, "My son, I don't remember."

I wept afresh as His forgiveness washed over me and I realized anew His faithfulness to forget and forgive my sins. Carol gave me a white rose, a crocheted baby blanket, and a small glass heart filled with oil representing my tears. We went outside and I released a white balloon to symbolize letting go and giving my child to the Lord. The beautiful ceremony really helped bring closure for me.

I slept with the little blanket under my pillow for a week. Now I have it on a shelf to remind me of my baby and God's forgiveness. I also wrote a letter to my baby but didn't share it at the memorial ser-

vice. It is between the three of us—me, my daughter, and the Lord. I started it with her lovely name:
My darling Redeemed…

■ Thinking It Through. ■

She's Right Here

You know a woman who has had an abortion. Since 1973 after the Supreme Court handed down the decision in *Roe v Wade*, half a generation has disappeared through pregnancy termination. The statistics are stark:

- 43% of American women will have at least one abortion in their lifetime.
- 47% of all abortions are performed on women who have had at least one previous abortion.[5]
- 22% of pregnancies in the U.S. (excluding miscarriages) end in abortion.[6]
- Though abortions have declined slightly in recent years, multiple sources record that approximately 1.2 million babies are aborted per year in this country. That's nearly 3,300 babies per day, or one every 38 seconds.
- Since 1973, more than 45 million children have not been born who would have been, and the repercussions on our economy are becoming clear.
- 1% of all abortions occur because of rape or incest; 6% of abortions occur because of potential health problems regarding either the mother or child; 93% of all abortions occur for "social reasons" (i.e. the child is unwanted or inconvenient).[7]
- Abortion is the most common medical procedure performed on women in the United States.[8]

In *A Solitary Sorrow*, author Teri Reisser puts to rest the idea that church-goers are less likely to know a woman struggling with abortion issues. "I have often been amazed by the number of the clergy who naively believe that few, if any, women in their congregation have had an abortion. Surveys have repeatedly demonstrated that the percentage of churchgoing women who have had abortions is the same as among the population at large."

Women don't brag about an abortion. They feel shame, deep sadness, guilt, and a host of other emotions they can't share. Unlike a miscarriage, in which the grieving woman is surrounded by others who wish to bring comfort and sympathy, an abortion is undertaken in silence, endured alone, and kept secret from friends or family who might normally be counted upon to help. This leaves a trail of victims beyond the children who never got the chance to be born and grow up—the women who aborted them, the men who often insisted on it, the peers and family members who made it "necessary" and even "convenient" for the woman to abort.

Many abortions are undertaken in an effort to save or maintain a relationship. A woman becomes pregnant, and her boyfriend demands she get an abortion because he refuses to support her and the child. A young girl has an abortion to keep from telling her parents and risk losing their love. A family has several children and can't afford another.

Unfortunately, in half or more of these situations, the relationship ends shortly after the abortion anyway,[9] leaving the woman to grieve both losses and question her choices. Though it seems the abortion will "solve the problem," in reality it introduces an entirely new set of issues and causes a fundamental relationship shift. If she does not receive counseling specific to abortion, a woman can linger in the throes of post-abortion syndrome for years, or even for the rest of her life.

Post-abortion Syndrome

Abortion is not a quick-and-easy solution. It is a painful, invasive, heart-wrenching procedure that prematurely ends the life of a child who would otherwise be born. No matter what the propaganda says, abortion leaves deep wounds on the soul of everyone involved.

Teri and Paul Reisser propose criteria for establishing post-abortion syndrome as a recognized condition in *A Solitary Sorrow*. Ramah International summarized the points on its website.[10]

- **Guilt**. A mother's primary instinct is to protect her children. For a woman who has an abortion, guilt can be crippling, especially if she was persuaded to go through with it by others, despite her own moral revulsion.

Jennifer: I definitely had guilt and still battle it sometimes. For a long time, I felt I didn't deserve to be a mother. I have not been able to conceive since the abortion. In the beginning, the guilt was completely debilitating. When it arises now, I speak truth to my heart: I am forgiven, God does want to give me the desires of my heart, I am clean in His sight. Since I blamed others (especially Seth) for the abortion, the guilt I felt was not as strong as it might be for another woman. In counseling, however, I came to grips with the fact that I'd made choices when I got into the cult: I chose to listen to Seth. I went to the clinic with Rhoda. I didn't feel I had a choice at the time, because I was so convinced I would go to hell if I left, and take everyone I came in contact with along with me, especially my baby. Now I know better, though it will probably always hurt.

- **Anxiety**. When extremely anxious, a person can experience physical changes such as heart pounding, stomach problems, headaches, and dizziness. Moods can swing wildly, and panic attacks are not uncommon. The anxiety arises from the conflict between the woman's personal moral code and the fact that she violated it in the most intimate way by having the abortion. To insulate herself, she may avoid anything to do with babies, from specific aisles at the grocery store to staying

away from friends who are pregnant or have
small children.

Jennifer: This has been huge for me. I used to get several panic attacks a day—or one that would continue all day. I was nervous and could not calm myself. I still get them but not frequently. I have married since I left the cult, and my husband prays over me and I read the Word aloud. It is possible they are from the abortion or from the entire cult experience, but they seemed to come back when we failed to conceive, so maybe it is more connected than I think. Prayer really helps, but sometimes I just have to ride it out, and say aloud, "God has not given us a spirit of fear, but of power and love and a sound mind" (2 Timothy 1:7, NKJV).

- **Psychological "numbing."** To avoid future pain, a woman may stuff her feelings deep inside and refuse to experience either joy or sorrow. This is part of what leads to the demise of many relationships after an abortion, when the woman walls herself off in self-defense. The results are depression and thoughts of suicide—from hopelessness to uncontrollable crying, sleep disturbances to outright suicidal thoughts. A study done by the Elliot Institute indicated 33% of post-abortive women surveyed reached a level of depression so deep they would rather die than go on.[11]

Jennifer: I talk about the abortion as the day I died emotionally and spiritually. I gave up all hope of God ever helping me, or of ever getting free of the cult. I resigned myself to a life of living hell to ward off, of all things, eternal hell. When I threatened to tell my mother what had happened to me, Seth lied and said she already knew. I almost committed suicide that day. The idea of leaving my mother alone in that place held me back. She was all I had left, even if she blamed me for the situation. The fact that Seth would lie about this never crossed my mind.

- **Anniversary syndrome.** Over half of post-abortive women apparently experience increased symptoms of PAS near the anniversary of the abortion or what would have been the due-date of the child.

Jennifer: I have more of an issue on the date I got pregnant—Labor Day, 2005. Since it is a national holiday, it is always a reminder.

- **Re-experiencing the abortion.** Either during routine gynecological exams or in dreams and flashbacks, many women continue to suffer from the abortion long after it is over. If the abortion was the type performed with suction, the sound of a vacuum cleaner can be very upsetting. Other sights and sounds can also trigger reactions.

Jennifer: My first visit with the infertility doctor brought on a flashback. I cried on the table. I worried the abortion caused my infertility. I had dreamed of a child knocking on my front door, and my counselor assured me this is normal. Spiritual and post-abortion counseling really helped. I would say that I still experience this to a degree when I go to the gynecologist or when I look on Facebook and see all the pro-life posts that are to bring awareness but actually bring on memories or flashbacks.

- **Preoccupation with becoming pregnant again.** Many women who have an abortion become pregnant again within a year, and may think of the new baby as a replacement for the one aborted.

- **Anxiety over fertility and childbearing issues.** The idea that she has aborted the only child she may ever become pregnant with haunts many post-abortive women. Another fear is that she may have a handicapped child as punishment.

Jennifer: Since childhood, I've desired to become a mommy. I went through a period of thinking I was unworthy of having a child, and that God would not give me one because of what I did. I have experienced major anxiety regarding not becoming pregnant, but that's also normal. I think the enemy wants us to believe God is against us so we grow apart from Him. I made a conscious decision to not be angry at God and not believe He was punishing me. I had to convince myself with my mouth, but I know He knows my heart's desire is to live by truth.

- **Interruption of the bonding process with present and/or future children.** Either refusing to risk being hurt again and holding her children at arm's length, or becoming an overly-protective mother can have negative results in a parent/child relationship.

Jennifer: I am happy to say that I am now a mommy to 5 amazing children. My husband and I were not able to have a child naturally so we became foster parents and we have adopted 5 beautiful children through the foster system. In the beginning I would say that I did struggle with holding on too closely or being over protective. However, time has brought healing and I know that my children are really the Lord's and He will protect them and one day we will all be reunited in Heaven.

- **Survival guilt.** An abortion is surrounded by intense pressure and life upset. There are myriad reasons a woman finally undergoes an abortion, but it comes down to a determination that she should live and the child must go. The immediate problem of the pregnancy is solved, but the woman may well feel incredible guilt for being the one "chosen" to live, at her baby's expense.

Jennifer: This is very true, but I can honestly say since I went through counseling, I don't have the guilt anymore. I am still sorrowful, but I know I am forgiven and can't rewind the hands of time.

- **Development of eating disorders.** A woman does not generally pick up her life and go on cheerfully after an abortion. The self-loathing can turn inward and become a subconscious need to be unattractive (either by weight gain or loss) and so avoid further pregnancy risk. To have some negative physical change after an abortion feeds a woman's need to punish herself for breaking her moral code. Weight becomes something she can control, in a life that feels increasingly out of control.

Jennifer: I simply didn't care anymore. I was overeating to an extent, and then Seth commanded that I gain fifty pounds as fast as possible to punish me. Once I had done that, I really felt disgusting and unworthy of anyone's attention or even friendship.

- **Alcohol and drug abuse.** Though they seem to numb the pain, the mental and physical side effects of drugs and alcohol actually intensify the problems with which the woman is already dealing.
- **Other self-punishing or self-degrading behaviors**—A woman may let herself fall into abusive or promiscuous relationships, hurt herself physically, or not take care of herself in basic and healthy ways.

- **Brief reactive psychosis**—Generally experienced within a few weeks of the abortion, the intensity of this reaction calls for immediate and compassionate professional intervention.

Jennifer: In a way, being in the cult protected me from some of these things. The kinds of behaviors some women fall into after an abortion went against my core beliefs. I was afraid of getting into further trouble or being beaten, so I didn't engage in any of it. I can completely understand how it would be an issue for some women, though. In my case, I got out of the cult and went straight into counseling. From the beginning of my counseling, I felt and experienced the Lord's forgiveness, so the self-destructive behavior never got hold of me.

Post-abortive women are all around us, suffering from some or many of the symptoms listed here. They agonize about the choice they made, dread someone discovering their secret, and need healing compassion to move on with their lives and connect with God again. Educate yourself about the issues and pray for opportunities to be the one a woman can open her heart to at last. The church should be the safest place for women to lay this burden down, but often isn't.

If you are post-abortive, get counseling. Make yourself vulnerable to someone you can trust and work through the issues that cripple your spirit. As Jennifer said, you can't turn back the clock, but you can move forward once again.

Resources

A Solitary Sorrow, by Teri Reisser and Paul Reisser, WaterBrook Press, 1999.
Real Choices, by Frederica Mathewes-Green, Conciliar Press, 1997.
Her Choice to Heal, Synda Masse, David C. Cook Publishing, 2009 (updated/expanded).
H.E.A.R.T. Manual: Healing the Effects of Abortion Related Trauma, by Heartbeat International.

Chapter 5

Breath of Freedom

I swipe a tissue across my forehead and stuff it back into my uniform pocket before heading to the floor to wait on the woman in the small booth in the corner. I want to gasp like a fish to urge more oxygen into my lungs. I breathe through my nose instead. Even here at work the odor of mold from the house Seth just moved us into lingers in my nostrils.

The woman in the booth is fanning herself idly with her menu when I approach. She smiles at me, but I only return a smaller version of that greeting.

"What can I get you today?" I hold my order book and pen at the ready.

She laughs. "A fan or an air conditioner would be nice. Where did this humidity come from?"

"I know what you mean. It makes it hard to breathe, especially when you have asthma." I don't mean to divulge information, but she's so friendly.

"You poor thing! And lugging all those heavy trays can't help. I'll keep your load light today. I just want a slice of peach pie and some iced tea."

I jot down her order and glance over the tables in the vicinity to see if anybody needs anything. Two men are chatting to her right. Parents are trying to keep their three small children coloring on their placemats to the left. The couple behind me is busy with their meal. All is well. I move away.

A shadow falls over my shoulder as I round the end of the counter to get the pie and iced tea. I am startled to see one of the men from the table next to my customer standing behind me. He fidgets with a belt loop on his pressed jeans, and the sun glints in his short brown hair. His eyes are kind and have laugh wrinkles forming at the edges.

"I'm sorry, Ruth." He doesn't need to read the name from my badge. He's been in several times before and remembers it. He has no idea it's not my name. I still jolt sometimes when I'm called by it, even after all these years. "I don't mean to interrupt your work, but I felt led to talk to you. I heard what you said to the lady over there about having asthma. Can I pray for you?"

My heart accelerates. Prayer is the only medicine I can take for my asthma, since Seth won't let me see a doctor.

He says it's the devil, and no doctor can cure it. After all, it's my fault for letting it in.

I look into his warm brown eyes and make a quick decision. "Yes, you can pray for me. But don't lay hands on me. I don't want any demons jumping from me to you."

Pause.

"Ruth, I'm a Christian."

Pause.

"I don't have to worry about demons. I have the Holy Spirit inside me. They can't jump on me. But I'll pray for you any way you like." He bows his head, and I hear him softly beseeching God for my healing as the clatter of dishes continues unabated from the kitchen.

"Father, you put concern in my heart for Ruth. This asthma is almost choking her, and I sense a powerful blackness in her left lung. Draw out the corruption in her lung and give her relief. Put Your hand on her, since I can't, and comfort her as You heal her. In Jesus' name, amen."

The customer looks up after his prayer and searches my face. "I feel such fear and anger in you. I don't know what is causing it, but I will continue to pray for you, that you will know the truth and not be afraid. I sense the Lord saying He's going to give you a time to release it soon." He tips his head up as though listening to someone's voice, then smiles gently. "Thanks for letting me pray for you. Sorry to intrude on your work." He turns smoothly and goes back to his table and his waiting friend.

The echo of his words swirls around my head with the chatter of the diner. The fact that he spoke words of knowledge over me is nothing new. Seth does it all the time. But something is different in this man's demeanor. His simple, confident statements resound inside me. Though I sway slightly, my feet are bolted to the floor. An electric current buzzes in my brain, louder than bees, more persistent than a ringing phone.

If you have the Holy Spirit, demons can't infest you.

My pounding heart nearly jumps out of my chest.

I hear it again. If you have the Holy Spirit… I blink rapidly…they can't infest you. Can't. Can't…

I know the ground beneath me is steady, but it feels as though it's vibrating.

I move somehow, despite the universe shifting around me. *Can it be true?* I think of all I've been taught by Seth for the past nine years. The endless hours of prayer binding the demons that seemed to lurk in every corner of my home and life. Seth's demands that I manifest all the demons living inside me that are waiting to try to attack him and others. The words of knowledge he's spoken to demonstrate their hold on me.

One or the other is true. They can't both be true. I stumble into the trashcan at the end of the counter. I want to crawl inside it and curl up to think until I am clear on this.

For now, there's iced tea to pour and a peach pie to slice, customers waiting for salt and ketchup, a booster chair to be fitted for a child. I move through my duties on autopilot, mulling my confusion.

At last, a break.

I step out the back door, and the sun hits me square in the face. The sky is blue, and I take a deep breath. Startled, I take another one. And another. My lungs feel like they could suck up oxygen forever. There is no pain on the left side. I continue to breathe in deep, greedy gulps. The words the customer prayed over me and spoke of my turmoil wash over my heart. *Could he be right?*

I reach into my pocket and fish out my keys, cross the employee parking area, and open my car door. From the back seat I fish out my Bible. I keep it in the car so Seth won't know I sometimes read more than just the passages he permits.

Lord, if it's true, prove it to me! My desperation makes me reckless, and I dare the God of the universe to perform for me.

Instead of a lightning bolt of judgment, I feel a tiny sweep of hope. I close my eyes and open the book. For a moment I'm afraid to look, afraid to be disappointed. At last, my eyes peek down. My finger is in Matthew 7, and I'm relieved the type is red. It is Jesus' words. Seth lets us read those most of the time.

"You will know them by their fruits. Grapes are not gathered from thorn bushes, nor figs from thistles, are they? Even so, every good tree bears good fruit; but the bad tree bears bad fruit. A good tree cannot produce bad fruit, nor can a bad tree produce good fruit. Every tree that does not bear good fruit is cut down and thrown into the fire. So then, you will know them by their fruits."

I think about prayer and easy breathing.

I think about berating and fear.

I recall the soft smile of the customer.

I imagine the angry red face of Seth as he demands I manifest demons I don't even know I have.

I think about fruit.

* * *

The receiver is slick in my hand, as usual. I'm glad I don't have a speaker phone—but then, tonight, I don't really need one. I would be able to hear Seth across the room.

"Now, tell me again why you were even talking to this man?" Seth breathes loudly in my ear, and I fear a quaver will give me away.

"I told you. He came in for lunch."

"Waiting on someone does not involve praying and exposing yourself to untold thousands of demons!" His voice rises in pitch, and I know if he were here he'd hit me. Hard.

"Please. Please." I don't know if I'm asking him to stop shouting or only to accept what I'm saying. Maybe both. Maybe I'm not even talking to him. "I was getting an order for a customer, and he started praying for me. I can't very well ask a paying customer to leave because of that." My whine makes me sick. Why can't I stand up for myself?

I explode in a spasm of coughing, doubling over to try to clear my breathing. The heavy smell of dampness and corruption seems to leach from the walls around me.

"That man is a demon. Your coughing is worse after his prayer than before. Obviously, he infested you further. And you let him!" I hear him throw something across the room at his end of the line. "Don't you realize these demons will take a year or more to get rid of? You are unutterably stupid! I don't think you're ever going to learn. I'm wasting my time with you. There are others who could do the work of the ministry a lot better than you, but I keep thinking you'll improve. Now I doubt you ever will." He sighs.

I expect him to hang up on me.

Maybe he'll throw me out. Maybe! The small kernel of hope I felt at the diner rises again but flutters back to the pit of my queasy stomach. The squeak of the chair he's sitting in comes clearly over the phone like the howl of an angry demon twisting back and forth in rage. As glad as I am he's not here, I know he wishes he were. My arm tingles like he actually hit me.

"It would be simple to throw you to the curb. I'd be done with you. But then I'd have to live with that the rest of my life. If I turn you over to your own sin and demons, you will go to hell, and take everyone you touch with you—you know that, don't you? You will be a walking plague. There isn't a person on the planet who will be safe from you. I would have to take the rest of the group somewhere else because we can't risk your infection. But even though you'd be out of my sight, I'd still hear your pitiful soul screaming for all eternity. And it would drive me crazy."

My mind looks down the dark, dank future he's painted for me. My vision blurs as a tear slips from the corner of my eye. I begin to shake. He'll take Mom away with him. I'll never see her again. And even if I could find them, I'd take her to hell with me just by getting in touch. I'm doomed if he lets me go.

"You've got a lot of work to do tonight to begin to get these new demons out of you. I'd suggest you get started.

I'll call you in a few hours and see how you've progressed. For now, I can't stand to have your voice in my ear. Even from this distance, you stink like a demon and reek of hellfire." He slams down the phone.

I crumple to the floor and hold my hand over my mouth, screaming and weeping. The clock in the kitchen chimes midnight. The clock in my heart stops entirely.

* * *

Kisses from Heaven

UNLIKE CULTS THAT ISOLATE THEIR MEMBERS from everyone outside their membership, we were free to come and go. In fact, it was necessary, since Seth needed us to earn a living and pay for things. Though we were not physically restrained, we were caged in even more intricate and exquisite ways by his voice in our minds warning us of hell and demons, damnation and loss. It was like being inside a high-voltage force field that would kill us or anyone nearby if we tried to step beyond it.

Waitresses can make good money if they have a popular restaurant to work in and are friendly. Since Seth would not allow friendliness, both my mom and I took double shifts at the diner to bring in as much as possible. Of course, our paychecks and tips went directly to Seth, so he could pay the bills. And sometimes he even paid them. Other times, they accumulated on my credit cards.

Seth favored our working double shifts. Not only did we bring home more pay, but exhaustion made us less likely to question or give him trouble. Often he called at eleven at night or later and kept me on the phone for hours dealing with demons in my life, and then I had to get up in a few hours and work another double shift. His demands and manipulation left us no time or energy to think.

I'm sure he assumed that with customers coming and going in a busy diner, there would be no chance of building relationships there, so we were effectively isolated even at work. But a neighborhood diner becomes a gathering place for people, a hangout for regular customers. For us, it became a lifeline to some form of sanity and hope.

Seth's physical abuse often left bruises or worse on me. A black eye or a broken bone was never beyond his power. I did my best to conceal them, and tried to come up with new excuses for "my clumsiness" when a new bruise had to be explained to coworkers and customers. Like most people hiding a secret, I thought others bought my stories, but certain customers took notice and began keeping a discreet eye on me. The man who prayed for me regarding my asthma was not alone in his concern.

One couple came in regularly. She was short and bubbly, with a ready smile and a laugh. He was taller, with thinned-out hair and strong arms. I got the impression he liked to work outside a lot. Because they always teased each other, I learned their names: Ira and Grace.

They came to the diner one day and ordered one of our specials, a fish plate. For some reason, Ira's plate arrived with an enormous portion. He was delighted, of course, and he insisted on returning to the diner over and over. This happened to him every time he came in! I certainly never asked the cook to add to the plate, or mentioned who it was for. But somehow, Ira always left the table more than satisfied.

Ira often asked for a table in my section. He and Grace became some of my regulars. I found it both unnerving and exhilarating that they seemed to care about me. They always noticed when I was limping or had a bruise or other signs of injury. Grace in particular looked me in the eyes each time, and I knew she hoped one day I'd let down my guard. For her protection, though, I could not.

After lunch one day she offered me her card. "Keep this," she said softly. "Call me any time if you need anything or want to talk."

I nearly choked over the lump in my throat, and panicked about what to do with the card. Finally, I memorized the number and threw it away so Seth would not find it. Engaging in that tiny act of defiance opened a small crack in the armor I'd worn for so many years. Small, yes, but it was a crack.

Rebellion shows itself in odd ways among people who've been repressed and forced into a corner for a long time. To one performing them, little actions take on huge significance if they've been forbidden and there's been punishment in the past. After nearly nine years in the cult, Mom and I both became a bit reckless in small ways, always worried Seth would discover our disobedience.

■ Engaging in that tiny act of defiance opened a small crack in the armor I'd worn for so many years. ■

We talked in the house together sometimes. -

Simply talking sounds innocuous enough, but Seth had strictly prohibited it. We'd been rebuked for it before, but how do you live inside the same four walls with your parent and never say a word? Silence was a unique kind of torture Seth had developed for us. We began picking the lock on our chain, one tiny word at a time.

We talked more freely in the car, since we felt safe there. We began to take drives so we could talk. Having obeyed the rule not to read the Bible except the book of 1 John and Jesus' words printed in red in the Gospels, we were completely ignorant about how to seek God's help in our situation. But we'd take the Bible with us in the car and open it at random and read something, even if it wasn't from the approved sections. Repeatedly, God graciously allowed us to come upon verses speaking of true freedom in Christ and the need to flee from evil.

As I wandered around in a nearby superstore on my break one day, I came across a book rack. The title facing outward had to do with spiritual warfare. I stopped dead. I looked over both shoulders to be sure no one I knew was watching me. My hand shook. I picked up the book, flipped it open, and read a bit here and there. It burned in my hands like glowing charcoal. I bought the book and hid it so I could read it later. It was a revelation, detailing not only the upside of spiritual warfare, but also how it could be taken to extremes and even abused to maintain power over other people. Though my heart pounded each time I opened it, the book drew me.

For the first time in years I began taking in and trying to process new ideas and viewpoints. I was bound to slip up and get carried away. One night Seth had me on the phone until the middle of the night, and I blurted out a question.

■ Though my heart pounded each time I opened it, the book drew me. ■

"Why do you say things like they're in the Bible, when they're not?"

Dead silence hung on the line for several heartbeats.

Then, "I didn't know you'd become a Bible scholar and memorized the whole book." His icy voice stabbed like needles.

I immediately realized my huge mistake. "I...of course I haven't. I just asked a question." I tried to keep the focus on the issue I'd raised, but I should have known better.

"And exactly where did you get this question? Frankly, it sounds way beyond your puny level of intelligence."

His mean laugh stiffened my back. "I read it in a book about spiritual warfare. It said the opposite of what you're saying. It bugged me, that's all." I tried so hard to be brave, hoping for a good outcome to this conversation.

"Really? And what book was this?" His purring voice frightened me more than a shout.

"Um...just a book I found somewhere. It doesn't matter. Never mind."

"Do you still have the book?"

I thought about lying, but I never had succeeded in getting away with it around Seth. "Yes."

"Do you have it right there?"

I ran my thumb over the cover, knowing it would be the last time. "Yes."

"I want to hear you tearing it up. Do you hear me? I am going to listen while you tear it completely apart and throw it in the trash. Now do it!"

My heart sank. I sobbed as I grappled with the thin book, pulling off the cover, then some pages, then some more pages. My hope dwindled with each tear. I could not bring myself to rip the pages into pieces, so I made a lot of noise pulling them apart. I threw the whole pile in the trash can.

Despite roadblocks like his discovery of the book, what Seth meant for harm and punishment turned out for our good. Mom went out to the trashcan, retrieved the bits and pieces of the book, and put it back together. Then she read about events in other countries that sounded as miraculous as what Seth claimed he could do. She realized Seth was not the only one who knew the Lord. She told me what she'd read, and it piqued my curiosity. I overcame my fear and read the book, as well.

■ What Seth meant for harm and punishment turned out for our good. ■

The book riveted me with its description of a leader who used the excuse of spiritual warfare to take control of followers' lives. He told them where to live, what car to drive, whom to marry, and even demanded sexual favors from them as a way of "getting rid" of their personal demons. It rocked us both. Mom began a quest to read more, learn more, question what we were being taught, and pray for confirmation of her growing conviction that we needed to get out. One page of our blossoming revelation turned to the next.

* * *

The cult wooed us slowly and carefully. The lies, manipulation, and false teachings encased us for over nine years. Yet when the end came, it came quickly.

Six weeks before we broke free, Seth beat me badly. As he pounded my head, I saw stars. I put up an arm to protect my head, and he hit that instead.

The next day I went to work with a swollen, discolored hand. I began with my usual excuses, but my coworkers convinced me to go to the hospital and have it examined. Seth had fractured a bone. An orthopedic surgeon set it. Though I continued to work, I couldn't lift the heavy trays, and customers noticed. Ira and Grace sat in my mother's section that day and asked her what happened to my arm.

She repeated the same lie I'd told, but it didn't sit well in their spirits. They said later it sounded like the devil trying to use someone to hurt me.

The fact that I'd sought treatment for my arm alarmed and enraged Seth. When his verbal berating stepped up a notch, I couldn't take it anymore.

"Leave me alone. If you don't, I'll tell my mother about what you did to me and the abortion you forced me to have." I knew that would put her over the top. Then she'd see we both needed to leave the group.

"Go ahead," Seth said in a mild, almost amused voice. "It won't be news to her. I told her awhile ago. She was fine with it."

The earth seemed to stop spinning.

She agreed? She didn't care that he made me give up the one thing I've wanted all my life—to be a mother? Her grandchild? I fell apart and began to weep. If my own mother didn't care about what had happened, I had no hope. She was the only person I thought I could depend on for love and support, and I was wrong.

"Why are you blubbering now? You wanted to run tell Mommy some big story and now you can't? Grow up! Get your head on straight, or I'll help you snap out of it. Yes, I told her. She doesn't want to discuss it any further, so leave her alone. If you disobey me in this, your reward will be hell, you know that."

How could my mother not stand up for me? How could she dismiss the life of her grandchild and the destruction of my life as well? A pit seemed to open in my heart, and I fell headlong into the darkness. I've never come closer to suicide.

■ How could my mother not stand up for me? ■

Seth would want me to stay in that pit, but the next day Mom drove me to work, since I could not drive with my arm in a cast. As we drove, she suddenly said, "I want you to know that I know what happened to you, and I don't agree with it at all."

My head came up and tears steamed down my face. A blaze of sunny hope shimmered inside me that has never been extinguished. She cared! She loved me! She supported me! She knew! Thinking she didn't mind what had happened to me was a greater trauma than almost anything else.

When Seth told her of our sexual encounters, the pregnancy, and the abortion, he'd made it clear it was all my fault. He tried to get her to hate me for being such a bad daughter and woman. He said I tried to bring him and his ministry down, but God would not let that happen. He claimed I didn't care for anyone but myself, and she should be glad she found out so she could guard herself against me. But she knew me far better than that. His obvious lies caused her to pull back far enough to take a good look at the true situation.

We spent the next few weeks comparing what Seth said with the Bible. Repeatedly we saw how the two did not align. At last we reached our scary decision: we needed to get away from Seth and his wife. We had nowhere to go, believed no one on the outside would remember us or want to hear from us. We would be launching off on our own, but at least we would be together.

October 7, 2007 became our declaration of independence day. We told Seth we would no longer be affiliated with his ministry. He raged and said we'd change our minds. We did not. We moved as quickly as possible, because Seth had threatened my life in the past. Though we locked the door, he still had a key. Every time the phone rang, we panicked.

■ October 7, 2007 became our declaration of independence day. ■

We searched ads in the paper for apartments, and drove past one. When we saw the outside of it we liked it, even though it would take longer to get to work than before. We both woke up the next day feeling we should go look at it, and we prayed for God's help. Making a decision frightened us. Almost a decade had passed since we truly exercised our wills in making our own choices. We prayed if God meant for this apartment to be ours, the doors would open wide and it would obviously be His work.

We loved the apartment but didn't have any money for the required security deposit. We'd scraped together just enough for the first month's rent. Prompted by something inside, we told the landlord our story.

"I would never normally do this, but I feel God wants me to rent to you. You can move this weekend, and just get me the security deposit by the end of the year," he said.

God had indeed kicked the door open for us. We felt His first kisses from heaven.

We sold everything we had except two boxes that went to Goodwill. We didn't want any ties to our past life, and Seth and Rhoda had picked out every bit of the furniture. Having a clean slate was awesome. We joked with the landlord that it wouldn't take long for us to move in, because we had nothing to bring. And God decided to drop kisses to earth on us again.

Our landlord offered to give us a bed and a desk. As he put them into the garage, a friend of my aunt arrived with two chairs he'd been storing for someone. They turned out to be our new landlord's old furniture and the friend a mutual one. He'd told the man to give them to whoever needed furniture. As his old items came full circle back to his apartment house, it gave the landlord peace about us.

Though we had jobs at the diner, we had no savings at all because Seth confiscated every dime he could. Again, God found a way to bless us. My grandparents had passed away before we entered the cult, but their affairs took a long time to settle. A year before we left the group, our family discovered the estate owed us some money. Our family and my aunt held the money for us. She'd left the cult some time before and told the family, "Save it. They'll need it when they get out." A few weeks after moving, we had $2,000 to praise God for, completely unexpected and undeserved.

People stepped in to help us left and right. When someone found out we'd left the cult, they'd come to the diner, and the celebration would begin all over again. A diner's daughter worked at a car dealership, and to ease our ability to get back and forth to work for our shifts she helped me to get a new car despite my bad credit. Each time an amazing event occurred, we marveled at the hand of God. It seemed He did all these things to reinforce that we'd made the right choice and that Seth was wrong. God's intervention on our behalf showed us we could depend on Him completely.

The fear of Seth finding us was palpable. I always had one eye on the rearview mirror when I drove. All he would have to do would be to follow one of us home from the diner, and he'd be able to make our lives miserable. We lived in an area with relatively small communities, so it was inevitable that we'd cross paths eventually. I knew I'd not be ready for it, no matter when it happened.

■ God's intervention on our behalf showed us we could depend on Him completely. ■

About two weeks after we left the cult, I stopped in at a local used furniture store to better fill our meager home. I stood looking at bedroom furniture, and suddenly he appeared immediately in front of me.

His face split in a knowing grin. "I knew you'd be here today."

No doubt my face lost all its color. Surely, he heard the pounding of my pulse. I don't know what I had expected to feel, but a roiling ball of anger, love, shame and fear welled up within me. I said a quick "Hello," turned, and hurried from the store. Once in my car with the doors locked, I fell apart and wept uncontrollably.

A few days after we moved out, Mom and I had begun counseling with Ira and Grace to deal with our experiences. Now I dialed their number. No answer. I punched in my aunt's number. She picked up, and I filled her ear with my sobs, regrets, and terror.

"Maybe I was wrong to leave. Maybe I should go back. I loved him. I betrayed him. How could I have done that? I was wrong to leave." I teetered on the edge of a precipice and could see no safe way down from the ledge.

My aunt prayed an incredible prayer over the phone. That settled me down enough to drive to the diner where Mom was working her shift. We huddled in the bathroom, and I cried as I told her what had happened. Then I sat in an empty area of the dining room because I didn't trust myself to get home on my own. I would wait for her to get off.

As I sat, I checked my phone for messages. I heard the one I'd waited years to hear.

After we'd escaped the cult, I had called my dad in California. I left him a message letting him know I'd left the cult and apologized for cutting off all ties to him. I asked his forgiveness but said I understood if he didn't call back. On this day, of all days in my roller-coaster-cult-exit, he phoned.

"Well, hello there!" his warm voice on the message reached out to me. "It's so good to hear your voice. There's no need to ask forgiveness. Call me any time."

While in the cult, I'd been taught to call Seth and Rhoda "Father and Mom." Seth had become a father figure in my life, among other things. That day, when I felt his pull most strongly, God had put my real father back in my life, allowing me to sever the rope looped around my heart trying to strangle me.

Living suddenly on our own felt like being released from prison without preparation or time for transition. Everything was new and scary. Small decisions seemed monumental. Going to the mall liberated, terrified, and overwhelmed us.

Simple things were brand new to me. I'd heard of MP3 players and other gizmos but had no idea how to operate one. The things I saw on television shocked me. Though we'd watched movies in our "ministry sessions," they didn't show the passage of time and moral disintegration like TV did.

Wearing makeup, deciding to diet, listening to music without worrying about it being confiscated, going out for dinner, going anywhere we wanted—all amazed me. We took a trip to San Diego to see my father. All I wanted to do was go to the beach. I stood with my bare feet on the sand, waves washing across them, and reveled in the sensation.

In the midst of liberation, fear dogged my steps. In the cult, we'd not been allowed to put our bare feet in the ocean because demons live there. We had rules about not sitting in another person's chair to protect us from demon transfer. According to Seth, birds brought demons; everything could bring disaster upon us.

But I fought the panic as my joy of liberation grew.

Moment by moment, day by day, turning off Seth's voice in our heads and enjoying life again became easier. I experienced setbacks and panic attacks, but I remained determined not to let Satan have any more of my life.

He'd already stolen ten years of it.

■ Thinking It Through. ■

You Can Be Free, Too.

If you are caught in a cult or spiritually abusive situation, you can be free, too.

Go back and read that sentence again.

How did this book come into your hands? Perhaps a friend gave it to you, or you found it somewhere, or you started out reading it in defiance-wanting to prove to yourself that your group is not manipulating you. You may keep it hidden, like Jennifer hid the book that started her quest for answers. If you are doing that, it says a lot; people in normal situations do not hide books.

If your heart quickened to read of Jennifer and her mother breaking free from the grip of Seth and his group, understand this is not a rare occurrence. People can and do break free all the time.

Maybe this is your time.

Breaking the bonds

When you became involved in the group or organization you're in, you probably moved in steps. You heard about the group, were skeptical, had some experiences with the group, began to get excited about it, and finally made a leap of faith and jumped in. As you can see from Jennifer's story, getting out is a lot like that. Small steps lead to a final, great leap of faith to freedom.

For Jennifer, it took nearly ten years of physical, spiritual and sexual abuse to force her to re-evaluate her life. Don't let it take that long for you.

Don't suppress your doubts about the group. Yes, you've gotten good at doing that, but just for this moment let the doubts wash over you. Let them play out in your head. What scares you? What is your greatest fear about leaving? Fearing to leave a group is not normal.

Give yourself permission to question-even if it's only in your head. Believe it or not, people in normal groups question things all the time. And nothing bad happens to them. They either reconcile their concerns, have someone explain it to their satisfaction or they move on. Questioning is acceptable.

Ask God to help you sort out the truth from the lies. Jesus said, "I am the way, the truth and the life" (John 14:6, KJV). As the creator and embodiment of all truth, He can lead you to a safe and nurturing place. Ask Him to show you what you need to know. Yes, you may have prayed a lot before you joined the group you're in. You may think God led you there, so how can you trust Him this time? If you're honest with yourself, you can look back and see how He tried to stop you from getting involved. Ask Him for guidance and be open to an answer from Him. It might take the form of a "chance" encounter with an old friend, a sudden new understanding of a Scripture passage or stumbling across a helpful and thought-pro-voking book (like this one.) Don't tell Him how to answer, or what you expect Him to do. He very much wants you to be free to live your life and worship in peace and joy.

Begin to make a conscious effort. Compare what is bothering you with what you know to be good and wholesome for your life.

When Jennifer examined the "fruit" of Seth's teaching, she saw it generated nothing but fear, paranoia, and isolation. She compared that to the wonderful freedom and healing she recognized in the words of the man at the diner. The disconnect between the two world views jolted her to think deeper. Thinking is not bad.

Evaluate what you are being taught in light of these new thoughts. Which path seems healthier to you? Which connects you to life and friends, family and society? It may be hard to face the fact that the teachings of your group are not geared to your best good, and in fact, are harmful. Don't shy away from the thought. Be an adult and face it.

Make a plan. It doesn't have to be a complete blueprint of how to exit your group. Decide what day you are leaving, where you will go first, and then go. Jennifer and her mom had no idea what reception they'd face when they left the group. They didn't know where they'd go once they were out. But they made enough of a plan to make it out the door. Life is uncertain. It's okay to take the first step onto solid ground and then wait to see the next step emerge in front of you. The first step is the important one.

Expect some "I told you so" when you get out. Rather than becoming defensive, why not just say, "And I agree with you now"? Let it go at that. Reintegrating into society, your family and regular activities will be a struggle. Think of yourself as a caterpillar that went into a cocoon for a while. Now it's time to fight your way out of the cocoon and become the butterfly you were always meant to be. When a butterfly wiggles and struggles to get out of its chrysalis, the effort forces fluids out into its wings, expanding them and making it possible for it to fly. Without the struggle, the wings will remain shriveled and the butterfly will never get off the ground. Expect the struggle, and welcome it as progress.

Connect with friends and family, but also look for people who have been where you've been. Not necessarily in the same group, but in a similar situation. Where do you find them? Be open with your story and they'll be attracted to you like iron filings to a magnet. You'll be amazed how many people have been through a cult-like experience.

Get on the Internet and make connections online with people all over the world. (Read their stories and comments with care.

Some cults lure people in through Internet contact, so keep your whereabouts to yourself, especially until you have a good comfort level with those with whom you are communicating.) In the Bible, Jesus foresaw that Peter would betray him in a weak moment. Rather than chastise him for it, Jesus told Peter the experience would work to his benefit and that of others. "But I have prayed for you, that your faith may not fail; and you, when once you have turned again, strengthen your brothers" (Luke 22:32). Draw strength from the struggles of others.

Resources

This book is in your hands for a reason. The concerns you've had about your group or organization may be completely legitimate. Don't stop questioning, seeking, thinking, praying until you find the path that will secure your steps. The first breath of freedom will be worth it.

Chapter 6

We Can't Do This Alone

I listen to the phone ring at the other end of the line. If she isn't there, it will be a sign.

"Hello?"

I feel both elated and terrified to hear that cheerful greeting. "Um…can I talk to Grace?" I know it's her already. I'm just stalling.

"This is Grace. Who's calling?"

"It's Ruth, from the diner." I hope she remembers.

"Ruth! I'm so glad you called." Her voice is gentle and melts over my heart like butter on a hot biscuit. "I told you that you could call any time. How can I help you?"

How can she help me? A torrent of answers floods my mind, but my tongue is dry. I look out the windshield across the parking lot to be sure Seth has not tracked me down like a wandering sheep and somehow gleaned that I am here making this call. I check the rearview mirror. Movement to the right catches my attention.

A hawk is circling high above. It wheels and loops through the beautiful blue sky. Another hawk joins it in its dance of joy. My heart skips a beat and suddenly I know what I want to say.

"Grace, we want to be free. I know you don't know anything about my mom and me, but we are trapped and we want to be free." My teeth close on my lower lip.

The sound of exhaled breath fills my ear and I can almost feel the warmth of it. "I have been praying every day that you would call, Ruth. The Lord impressed on my heart that you are in a dark, dark place. You are in bondage to something. I don't know any details, but my sense of your fear and sadness is so strong. I've been waiting for you to call so I can pass on a message from God to you: He is light. In Him there is no darkness. He loves you very much, and is eager for you to step back into the light again."

I can't brush away the tears fast enough, and finally just let them slide off my chin and onto my blouse. "Can you help us, Grace?"

"Ira and I are nobody—but we stand hand-in-hand with a mighty God, and He can help you. We're here any time you need to talk. Please come see us."

The hawks each reach the farthest extent of their circling patterns, and turn to race back toward each other. From my vantage point, it appears they nearly collide. But I know they are rejoicing in the currents, letting the cool breeze ripple through their outspread feathers, and my soul takes flight at last.

Hope, long denied, is nearly a physical force when it closes around my heart.

* * *

Mom and I wait for our knock to be answered. I doubt I've spent more than an hour or two away from her in the few days since we've left Seth's group. We're like two trees blown against each other by a horrific wind, and can no longer stand on our own unsupported.

The door opens and Grace's wide smile flashes as she draws us inside. It's a comfortable home, open and welcoming. Something warmly fragrant wafts from the kitchen. Ira looms over her shoulder, a large, reassuring presence with kindly eyes.

We pause inside the door, surprised to see three other women. Mom and I exchange a worried glance.

"Welcome to our home," Grace touches my back momentarily to bring us farther inside. "This is our daughter Gerry, and friends Carol and Barb. They're here to help us pray together and minister to you—but if you'd rather they leave, they will."

I didn't expect an audience for this! Fear tingles from my chest to my fingertips. Yet something like peace brushes my mind and I accept them as part of the spiritual resuscitation team. Another glance at Mom tells me she feels the same conflicted feelings. I let the peace win out.

"No, that's fine," I hear myself say. "Though I don't know if they will want to hear what we have to say." My eyes drop. "It's a pretty ugly story."

Grace looks deep into my eyes. "God can give you back beauty for any ashes that have burned through your lives."

It is the second time she has spoken truth to my confused mind. I know it will not be the last.

* * *

A heavy purple silence wraps itself around the table where all seven of us sit. No one moves, even to wipe away the tears that wash several cheeks, including mine. I am exhausted.

On the way here, Mom and I agreed this counseling would not be of any use if we held back. "We must be completely honest and tell them everything," she'd said. "You must tell them what happened to you. All of it."

They are stunned.

I wish it could have been a simpler story with fewer convolutions. But it now hunches on the table between us like a gargoyle. The lies, the fear, the abuse. I told them all the things Seth convinced us of, and the terror we still harbor that he might actually be right. Endless days of binding demons in every corner of our lives. Endless nights of berating phone calls. The money we handed over to Seth. The control we allowed him to have. The sexual abuse, the abortion. It is a frightful pile of filth to have spilled out in front of them, but we did it.

Now I am numb. I want to hold Mom's hand under the table as we wait for their response, but a decade of prohibitions die hard.

Ira exhales air from between pursed lips and blows his nose. His gaze travels around the table. "I think we need to pray some more before we go one step further."

They didn't turn away from us. My heart resumes beating again.

Grace's voice is whisper-quiet and ragged. "Father, though You know every detail of Jennifer and Marian's story, we've just heard it for the first time. We're crushed by the things that have happened to them, but know You are already moving to heal and to rework these experiences for Your glory. There is much that needs to be addressed, much that cries out for correction, much that we are having a hard time absorbing. So we turn to You and put our hands over our mouths. We ask that Your Spirit would guide us and show us where to even begin. This is an enormous, complicated, tightly-tied knot. But You are the God who knows just which thread to pick up first and how to unwind it and unbind it from them. Use us as Your instruments. Be the Mover and the Healer in this circle. In Jesus' name, amen."

As she prays, a sliver of warm light penetrates my dark heart. It is the first light I have seen in years and I am momentarily blinded by its brilliance. I begin to weep again in earnest.

Mom's eyes fill with tears and I know the light of hope has risen in her heart, as well. I know we both want to step into that light and never leave it.

* * *

Emotional recovery room

LEAVING SETH'S GROUP WAS A MILESTONE IN OUR LIVES and our spiritual journey, but only the first step in a very long road of recovery. I think we both sensed that if we did not ground ourselves in the truth, completely different from his teachings, we would risk sliding back—as he predicted we would. Within days of exiting the cult, we were counseling with Ira, Grace, and the rest of their prayer team. Looking back, it's clear this played a vital role in our healing.

Agreeing to be completely honest about what we'd been through also became key to our healing. Had we held back or delayed telling the "worst" parts (how do you determine what is worst in such a situation?) it would have slowed our ability to process and recover from the error we'd lived in for ten long years. It was embarrassing, humiliating, painful and shocking. Though we'd lived every moment of that decade a day at a time, to recap it for others in the space of a few hours frightened even us.

If any of the five counselors had pushed back from that table and said, "Sorry, this is beyond us. We can't help you. Go find a therapist," we would have been devastated.

Instead, they recognized their own limitations in addressing our specific needs and went to God for direction.

From the start, they advised us to cut ourselves off from Seth and others in the group completely. They knew we remained vulnerable to the pull of deception. Other than the one encounter I had with Seth at the furniture store, we have we have only seen one non-family member from the cult since we left it. This has been a blessing. In the beginning, we feared Seth. We'd seen him pray curses against people who left the group, and knew he was doing the same toward us. We couldn't guess what he might do if he actually discovered where we lived and decided to make life difficult.

Though we felt compelled to share the physical conditions and much of the spiritual deception we'd experienced, some of the teachings were so ingrained in us that the idea of voicing them frightened us. What if Seth and Rhoda were right? Wouldn't speaking against them be the same as blaspheming the Holy Spirit?

Seth and Rhoda believed they were key people mentioned in the Bible, with an important role to play in the End Times. We wanted Ira and Grace to understand what we'd been taught, but couldn't bring ourselves to describe this teaching aloud.

I came at the subject carefully. "You know, the people in Revelation chapter eleven?" That was as close as I could come to voicing it.

Grace turned to the passage and read it, a puzzled look on her face. "I don't understand. What do you mean?"

"The people in that passage… Seth and Rhoda think…"

Mouths dropped open around the table. "They think they're the two Witnesses from Revelation?"

It was a relief that someone besides us said it, but now it was out. If they truly were the two Witnesses, they had great power. We'd been taught to believe they could literally breathe flames and send us to hell for going against them.

"Jennifer, Marian, that is not true." Barb's voice was gentle but insistent. "They are not these Witnesses. They don't fit the qualifications. Neither of the Witnesses is a woman. The Witnesses are not raised up until the great tribulation period. Believers are not in it; we've been raptured by then. The Witnesses are not going to live as two Americans running a cult and working the night shift at a supermarket."

The five of them linked their hands with ours and began to pray for the cleansing of our minds from each false teaching Seth had planted there. They asked God to protect us from our own thoughts until we grew strong enough to think clearly. They prayed for peace and a renewed spirit of truth in our lives. We would repeat the process many times. As our counseling uncovered error, truth was spoken over it and we were set free.

Healing spiritual damage is a gradual process, just as we acquired the wounds in slow steps. Even now, years after the cult lost its grip on us, I still struggle with the Bible. Seth used it like a club to beat us into submission, twisting verses for his own use. When I come across them now as I read, or hear them from the pulpit, it's hard not to immediately click back to the thought patterns I had when I first heard them.

In a way, they are like smells. A single "sniff" can trigger whole hours or days of memories.

■ I still struggle with the Bible. Seth used it like a club to beat us into submission. ■

* * *

Another part of our counseling and recovery centered around two aspects: confession and forgiveness. Even though we had been abused, there were things we could have done differently to either escape it or avoid it entirely. We made choices to join and stay with the group. Each of us needed to take responsibility for our own actions. If we didn't, we would always be victims, blaming Seth and Rhoda or others, and never be free.

At the beginning of my cult experience, from my first meetings with Seth and Rhoda, something told me they were wrong. Yet I overcame that reluctance because of the flattering and exciting "prophecies" Seth spoke over me. As things went along, I chose to believe things even though the Holy Spirit prodded me, telling me it was wrong. I had a Bible, but I chose not to believe the verses that said God loves me, and He will never forsake me. Instead I listened to Seth until he convinced me that God hated everything about me and would be perfectly happy if I ended up in hell. I read what Seth told me to read and tuned out the rest. I chose to do that.

I confessed my role in embracing the deception in the first place and then letting it continue for ten years. I admitted my attraction to Seth over time, and my responsibility for letting things evolve as they did. I faced the fact that I could have taken Mom's hand, led her to the car, and driven us both away—any time during those ten years. It was a wrenching period of counseling as we both dealt with this side of the equation.

■ I confessed my role in embracing the deception. ■

Forgiveness is a two-sided coin. I needed to ask forgiveness from many people, and I got to work on that within a week of exiting the cult. People had tried to stop me from getting involved, and I'd ignored them or told them off. I'd pushed my husband away and allowed him to divorce me so I could be in the group. I'd not spoken to any of these people in ten years. I had no idea what to expect when I began contacting them, but I knew I had to do it for the success of my own recovery and to put closure to that time of my life.

Though my husband had walked away when I chose the cult over him, he had told me that he hoped I got out some day.

"I don't care if I'm remarried. If you ever get out of that group, you call me. I want to know you're all right." He'd left the door open a crack, and I hoped it would still respond if I pushed on it.

I got in touch with him through his sister-in-law. We had an incredible conversation. He was very nice to me, despite what I'd put him through. He is remarried and happy. He asked me to forgive him for not trying harder to help. I admitted nothing he could have done would have stopped me. I asked his forgiveness, and he graciously gave it. He wished me well, and together we put closure to the dangling bits of our old marriage.

Others I needed to ask forgiveness of included friends who'd tried to talk sense to me, family members who watched first my aunt, then my mother and sister, and finally me being swallowed up by the group. Nearly all gave a warm response and genuine forgiveness for my wrongs against them. Our freedom elated them.

Each time I picked up the phone, I had to remind myself, "Your name is Jennifer." Seth had changed it to Ruth, using the excuse that this was a common practice in the Bible when God got ready to use someone. I had a hard time resuming my correct name. Again, if the name change came from God, who was I to undo it? I feared He would reject me if I took back my old name. Counseling helped me to see only God has the right to change my name. Seth was not God.

I continued to work at the diner as a waitress. One regular customer was a pastor. We often had good conversations, though I never mentioned my cult involvement. Two weeks after we got out, he came to the diner and sat in my section. "I need to introduce myself to you," I said, sitting at his table. I put out my hand. "My name is Jennifer."

He laughed, thinking I was joking with him.

"Really. My name is not Ruth. My mother and I have been in a cult for ten years, and we just got out of it. I am meeting you now for the first time as the person I really am. My name is Jennifer."

To my amazement, he began to sob. "I sensed something wrong in you and prayed for you many times. Recently I've had a difficult time with my church. I told God today that I wanted to go Home. I have no reason to go on." He wiped his eyes. "Then He had you come to my table and tell me what you said. It shows me God does answer prayers, and He is in control. God is so good! I think I can go on now."

Coworkers and customers noticed the changes in our demeanor. What they saw gave a testimony to the power of God to restore broken people. Suddenly we were light and free, rather than downtrodden and frightened. As regular customers came in, they rejoiced with us in our new life. I discovered that no one had believed my stories of "falling" or "walking into things" to explain my bruises, black eyes, and broken bones. They knew abuse when they saw it, but our way of holding people at a distance had kept them from intervening.

■ Suddenly we were light and free, rather than downtrodden and frightened. ■

* * *

Another lovely encounter came with one of our past landlords. Seth always had us live in farmhouses or other places at a distance from others. We lived at a dairy farm for six years, assuming no one could tell there was anything unusual about our situation. Again, we were wrong; people are more perceptive than we thought.

Our landlords wrote us a letter while we lived on their dairy farm saying they sensed something was wrong. They worried that Seth was a cult leader, and told us, "If you need help, we're here. We can help you get a temporary restraining order to keep him away, or whatever you need."

Of course, we had to tell Seth about the letter. We moved immediately after that.

As the Lord brought this kind couple to my mind, I recognized another situation for which I needed to ask forgiveness. I called them, explained who I was, and asked their forgiveness for how we treated them. I told them we were out of the cult now and thanked them for praying for us. Later they came to the diner to see us, and even gave us $100 to get a new start. It was a warm blessing from the Lord to feel the years of hurt and pain sloughing off like an old skin.

* * *

The other side of the forgiveness coin came much harder. It involved extending forgiveness to those who had hurt and misled us.

There are two kinds of forgiveness. The extension of grace to cover a wrong when the person who committed the wrong asks to be forgiven is one type. Each time I asked people from my past to forgive me, they extended and blessed me with that loving grace. But what about when the people who hurt you don't ask for forgiveness? In the case of Seth and Rhoda, I truly don't expect they ever will—though all things are possible with God. Should they be forgiven when they've not asked?

Hurting another person is like stretching a rubber band between the two of you. When the hurt is raw and fresh, the band is tight. Often it snaps and leaves you stinging. Though time may pass, the band never really dissolves until it is dealt with. It remains ready to tighten and lacerate your heart in a flash. If one person asks for forgiveness and the other extends it, it is like lifting that rubber band from around the two of you and tossing it where it can't cause damage any more. But if the person who put it around both of you in the first place doesn't wish to be forgiven, there's nothing to do but cut it and free yourself.

Unforgiveness is a shackle. Even if you never see the person who hurt you again, you go on snapping the band of that unforgiveness and hurting yourself until you get rid of it. We set out to break the shackles of blame and bitterness that still held us captive. Though Mom and I went to counseling together for the first three months, gradually we began to go separately so we could deal with our individual issues more openly. This was important, because we both needed to express our anger about the role the other had played before we could ask each other for grace.

■ Unforgiveness is a shackle. ■

Ira, Grace and the prayer team asked if I felt I could forgive Seth and Rhoda for what they'd done to us while we were in the cult. I certainly did not feel like doing so, but I saw the importance of cutting that tie. I knew this forgiveness would have to come from God, and He would have to help me through it.

First we prayed through prayers of forgiving them for all the ways they'd hurt us, abused us, lied to us, and for taking my baby. It was hard. I cried and cried and cried. It was the first step in a journey of letting it go. I have had to cut the tie of unforgiveness many times where they are concerned, but each time it gets a little easier, the past a little more distant and indistinct.

I needed to forgive my aunt, the first in our family to be pulled into Seth's net. My mother had followed her, and I held a lot of resentment because she didn't do more to stop me. My sister and her husband had gotten out of the cult before we did, though they had not gone through a healing process. I felt angry my sister didn't do more to try to pull us out. I had a long list of people I blamed. Confronting that list showed me I needed to again take responsibility for my own actions, and let go of the resentments holding me back. This period of our healing proved vital to our mental and spiritual health. Without it, I doubt we'd be where we are today.

We began meeting with the prayer team twice a week, then eased back to once a week. Finally I only called them for counseling when issues cropped up we couldn't deal with, or I hit a plateau and needed a fresh nudge, or panic attacks kicked in. Sitting with these godly people, surrounded by their acceptance and love, and wrapped in prayer was a beautiful experience. God used them as His arms to hug us, His shoulder for us to cry on, His hands to applaud our progress.

Some of our friends were alarmed to hear about our counseling with Ira, Grace, and the others so quickly after leaving the cult. "You've just replaced one dominating personality with a group of them!" they said, worried for us all over again.

Though it might look like that from the outside, it is the fruit of the relationships we built that shows its value. I explained there were huge differences between counseling with our prayer partners and being under Seth's control.

Seth used Scripture to keep us in line. Our friends opened the Word to us, put the verses back into context for us, and let us read them ourselves. We experienced the love of God first hand by reading His words.

Seth made rules and threatened us with hell fire and exile if we didn't comply. Ira and Grace gave us sensible, biblical guidelines for our own good. We'd lost the ability to make decisions after not making any for so long, and we needed some help. They left it up to us to choose whether we'd follow their advice or not.

Seth dominated our every moment. From waking to sleeping, and even dealing with dreams, he was the ever-present authority. He commanded when to eat, where to sit, what to think. The prayer counselors encouraged us to rediscover our own thoughts and wishes, our own dreams and spiritual life. They were in the business of picking the locks on our hearts, rather than looking for more chains to contain them.

Because of the abortion, I also went beyond our prayer circle and spent time with my professional therapist to deal with the aftermath of that situation. I will never forget her gentle methods and compassionate massaging of my heart.

Regaining one's footing after being in a cult, abusive relationship, or similar situation is a process. While it might be possible to undergo that transformation alone, I am certain my mother and I are as strong and free as we are today because we asked God to help us. He sent people to form a chain from the bank of the river to the swirling rapids to reach out and help us to shore. They weren't afraid to get wet.

■ Thinking It Through...■

Breaking New Trails

When a person ends a relationship and promptly becomes romantically involved with someone else, we say they are "on the rebound." Such relationships rarely last and usually cause a good bit of pain to both parties before they end.

Leaving a cult is much like a marital break-up. The same ties that cause a shredding of the heart when the dissolution finally comes can cripple the ex-cult member, leaving him or her vulnerable to filling the vacuum with the first strong-willed person or group that comes along. Many people who exit cults end up either back in the same cult or in another one, unless something is done to break the pattern of dependence that has developed in the course of cult membership.

Leaving an abusive group or cult is a process. There may be a specific day and moment when the break actually comes, but prior to that action and following it are many steps if the member is to readjust successfully to society.

Upon leaving the cult, Jennifer and her mother made an unusual decision. They agreed to be open about their experience. You probably know people who have been in cults, but you don't realize it because they've stuffed the experience down and refuse to admit it. It's shameful to them and a sign of bad judgment they'd rather forget. Though this has gotten them past the experience itself, it has probably stunted their ability to process it and move on in a healthy way.

If you are leaving an abusive group, make up your mind that you will not deny the reality of what's happened to you (and your role in it). If you are reaching out to someone who has exited (or would like to exit) a cult, gently but firmly encourage them to talk about what has happened and address the issues involved. It is the best way to truly put it behind them, and the only way to mine the gems of wisdom that such an experience brings.

For the person who leaves a cult and is alone, it can be a daunting task to find support. If this is you, know that your feelings of fear, indecision, doubt, and loneliness are completely normal for where you are in the process. You've not been able to take control of your life for some time. Suddenly, it is all in your hands. For some, like Jennifer and her mother, this sudden burst of freedom proves both breathtaking and paralyzing.

Where can you turn for help? Who can you trust? You trusted someone with your very soul for a long time-only to find that trust misplaced. Reluctance to trust again is normal. There are churches all around, but which are right? How do you find a counselor or group of people to talk to, like Jennifer did, who will not condemn you or cause you further pain?

In the beginning, you'll feel raw and exposed. People are intimidating, even threatening. So take it slow and perhaps start with the more impersonal ways to begin your healing. Books can be very important. They don't judge, they just provide information, and often lead to further resources that will be helpful to you. The internet can be a lifeline-though it must be approached with caution. Reputable sites can put you in touch with counselors who can even work with you online, or refer you to experienced people in your area.

Resources

The resources listed here are a place to start. Reading will provide insights into your cult experience, and help in returning to a more balanced and healthy mindset. Many have bibliographies at the end, stepping stones to your next discoveries.

Churches that Abuse and Recovering from Churches that Abuse, both by Ronald Enroth, Zondervan.

Recovery from Cults: Help for Victims of Psychological and Spiritual Abuse is a series of chapters written by the top experts in the field of cult recovery, and edited by Michael D. Langone, W.W. Norton Company.

Take Back Your Life: Recovering from Cults and Abusive Relationships, by Janja Lalich and Madeleine Tobias, Bay Tree Publishing, Berkeley, California.

Spiritual Abuse Recovery: A Recovery Workbook for "Friendly Fire" Casualties, by David Henke. This workbook includes information, Scripture, interactive questions, and resources for further study. [In the interest of full disclosure: I helped edit the workbook.] It is available from Watchman Fellowship, a ministry of spiritual discernment,(706) 576-4321, <u>dhenke@watchman.org</u>.

Out of the Cults and Into the Church: Understanding and Encouraging Ex-cultists, by Janis Hutchinson, published by Kregel Resources.

Getting your hands on quality materials to help you begin to put your life back together is a first step, and a crucial one. Eventually, you'll want to progress beyond that point. The resources listed here will assist you in making those next steps.

How do you know when you're "done" healing? Is there a tape stretched across the finish line you can eventually break through? It's a valid question.

In his Spiritual Abuse Recovery workbook, David Henke includes a Recovery Scale that may be helpful to measure where you are today, and where you can aspire to be in the future. He has given us permission to reproduce it here.

No matter where you may be on the scale, look at it as an indicator of where you can be in the future.

Then take a step. One is all it takes to start the journey to wholeness once again.

Recovery Scales

Every individual's recovery from spiritual abuse and deception is unique. Your journey back to spiritual, emotional and personal wholeness may take or years—yet it will happen, if you work at it. Along the way, you'll wonder how you're doing. The scale below can give you a gauge of how far you've come, and encourage you that the remaining steps are possible. You may not complete all the step, or in this order, but you CAN recover.

Where are you on the scale today?

Bondage

15. I am involved in my group and happy.
14. I am beginning to feel discontent with questions and confusion.
13. I have serious thoughts about leaving the group.
12. I am preparing the exit the group.
11. I have broken with the group.
10. My new life has begun (job, home, daily routine, spiritual quest.)
9. I have begun receiving counseling
8. I am making new friends.
7. I am seriously and honestly evaluating my experiences.
6. I have found a supportive community

5. I am trying new churches
4. I have settled into a church
3. I have processed my experiences to the point of being able to help others.
2. I have forgiven the abusers and myself.
1 Positive spiritual experiences have become the norm.

FREEDOM

What steps can you take to move ahead?

Reprinted from *Spiritual Abuse Recovery: A Recovery Workbook for "Friendly Fire" Casualties,* by David Henke with his permission.

Chapter 7

Here Comes the Bride

The motel is not in the better part of town. It's not even in the less desirable part of town. It's seedy and small. The rooms open directly onto the sidewalk bordering the parking lot that runs from the office to the ice machine. Seth pulls into a space in front of a room and turns off the engine. He gets out without hesitation and draws a young man out of the vehicle after him. He knocks on the door of a particular room and Rhoda opens it. They step inside. Jennifer's attractive younger sister, Janice, rises, clutching her hands together.

"Meet your wife," Seth says, as the other man falls back a step. "Just like your dream, here she is, at this motel, this very room." Janice and Phil peer at each other in the dim gloom.

"We'll have the wedding in a few days, but for now, let's go get something to eat." Seth, it seems, is always hungry.

* * *

"Oh, Aunt Carolyn, they're lovely," Janice says, lifting the colorful bouquet from the older woman's hands. It will give her something to hold on to so her own hands won't show their shaking. A bridal bouquet, a motel room, and a man she only met a few weeks ago. She needs something to clutch.

"Let me see those." Seth snatches them from Janice's hands and turns to the top of the dresser. He sets the flowers down and begins removing various bits of greenery, flowers, and ribbons. When he is done, twelve now-bedraggled white flowers remain of a fifty-dollar display. "There, for the twelve tribes of Israel. Perfect."

He hands the ugly floral disaster back to Janice and they turn as a knock announces the arrival of the minister. Though Seth plans to perform the ceremony, the minister will make it legal. The confused, black-suited man steps into the strangest wedding in which he will probably ever take part.

* * *

"I've found an apartment for you, but it doesn't have furniture, so we need to get some." Seth sighs tiredly. He turns into the lot of a discount furniture store. The women begin to gather their handbags in order to go into the store. Seth shakes his head.

"You all sit tight. I'll be right back." He puts out his hand for Janice's credit card.

They watch silently through the large plate glass windows as Seth weaves his way among the various furniture groupings. A salesman approaches, and Seth points at various items. They move to a desk to complete paperwork and payment.

Seth slides back behind the wheel fifteen minutes later. "Here," he says, handing Janice her credit card. "It will all be delivered in a few days. I gave them your new address. Let's go there now, and I'll tell you where I want you to put things."

No one says a word as he drives to the outskirts of town, far from convenient shopping, possible employment, and medical services. Seth points out a bus stop several minutes before arriving at the apartment building. When he drives away, he takes their only form of transportation with him.

* * *

Family affair

I GOT INVOLVED IN SETH'S MINISTRY despite my misgivings because everyone I trusted or looked up to was already

98

wrapped up in it. My aunt and my mom were first, but my younger sister, Janice, followed them. By the time I got involved, there was already a lot going on I didn't know about. Seth withheld the real reason he moved my younger sister to California—to marry a man she'd never met to further the work in the ministry there. The truth came out awhile later.

Though all my immediate family were pulled into Seth's ministry, we each came to the group differently, and all suffered alone. Though my sister and mother were involved in the cult, our isolation from one another kept us from knowing each others' hearts.

Janice's Story-Through a Sister's Eyes

I partied in high school and through my junior year in college. I got good grades, even graduated on the Dean's list, but didn't live for God in any way. My best friend and I decided to start living less wild during our junior year. We quit smoking, didn't go out as much, and started attending a great church. Things were looking up. I grew hungry to know more about God and developed an interest in missionary work. Though my friend planned to join a particular evangelistic ministry when she graduated, I had no specific goals.

I wound up a few credits short for graduation and had to go an extra semester. During the summer preceding my last few classes, I lived at home. My mom and aunt became more involved in spiritual things, and I enjoyed the fact that we seemed to finally have something in common. We went to see evangelists together, and my aunt took me to a women's conference some distance away. During the drive she told me about Seth and Rhoda, describing how they took her under their wing from the first time she went into their store, and said they offered a deliverance ministry. Considering all the things I had done wrong in my short life, I felt I needed to be set free from a lot. I thought God was leading me to be healed from the junk in my past. I wanted to feel fresh and clean again.

I went to their store one evening after closing time. They had Christian music playing in the background and gave me a soft drink. They never mentioned money. It all seemed legitimate.

Seth asked me a series of questions, and I told him everything about my past. It felt so good to tell someone things I'd never really admitted aloud before. Then he led me through a prayer to rid myself of all the demons that had taken control of me because of my sinful behavior. He cut off what he called "soul ties and bondings" to the people involved. I felt weird, and at one point my body jerked. Seth said the demons were leaving me. He prophesied over me and told me how much God loved and cared for me. I felt strange, different, scared—but it all seemed good. After all, how could I judge people of God?

■ It felt so good to tell someone things I'd never really admitted aloud before. ■

I told my friend about the experience, and one evening we both went to see Seth and Rhoda. He gave my friend an awesome prophecy that her fiancé had a huge calling on his life, and she'd be a praying wife in support of his ministry. (As it later turned out, her boyfriend left her before the wedding.) Seth also prophesied in a less positive vein over me. He said I would have to suffer for Christ. He gave us both prayers to pray so we could cast out demons and cut off "soul ties." I grew terrified to come in contact with people, or for people to call me, because then I would have to cast out demons and sever soul ties again.

I had a boyfriend when I began counseling with Seth, but they didn't get along. In fact, my boyfriend accused Seth of being crazy and walked out of the meeting. He wasn't open to all the talk about dealing with demons through spiritual warfare. It disappointed me, because I liked him. Seth said he was not the man God wanted me to be with. In one of our counseling sessions, Seth said a "word" came to him about who I was to marry. He verified the insight with Rhoda, and they said the man had joined their ministry already. They described him as a strong follower of God who had moved to California to prepare for a music ministry. The prophecy excited me. I longed to be active for God. I'd been praying for such a man of God to be my husband.

Seth said "Phil" and I would be forerunners of God and the ministry in California. I would be taken to my husband like Rebekah had been taken to Isaac in the Bible. Though some of that scared me, I thought it was also really cool to be part of something so grand. I began to fast and pray. I read the story of Isaac and Rebekah, asking God what to do. I sensed God telling me to change my name to Rebekah. Seth and Rhoda confirmed the name change before I said anything. I told Seth I would go to California. He seemed a bit shocked at first but recovered and said God had already told him I would.

I moved in with Seth and Rhoda for a few weeks before going to California so Seth could train me spiritually for my role. I had to be pure to meet my husband. In reality, this became a time of hardcore brainwashing. Seth stayed constantly by my side, filling my mind with the ministry we would have. God planned to do something new, and we would be His vessels to bring it about. Seth said I would sing like an angel and play guitar—I had always wanted to do both. Phil would play drums after being taught to do so in the spirit by angels.

I learned many thrilling things. Seth had been made God's true prophet, the Father of this generation. He would judge nations. He would be able to kill with his breath and his words because the judgment of God was coming soon. I was on the winning side. We would all have new bodies then.

The prophecies enticed me.

It was personally costly to delve into the spirit realm as deeply as Seth and Rhoda's ministry did. They said their new level of warfare scared the demons with its intensity, terrifying Satan. Seth came under regular attack, either because of demons or because of my own sinful wretchedness. Along with the interesting prophecies came continual rebukes for my lack of diligent preparation. I kept thinking I just had to get through the training process. Once I reached California and got away from direct contact with Seth, I assumed I would not be so severely watched and punished. I was very wrong.

■ It was personally costly to delve into the spirit realms■

I gave Seth and Rhoda all my clothes and belongings, including my car, so they could sell them and help pay for my plane ticket. These things had hordes of demons living in them, so they had to go. I had already thrown out books, music, photos, and jewelry—the final clean-out represented one more step in the purging process. We went to a cheap discount store to buy new clothes. Nothing too tight, too low, just boyish and plain. I couldn't wear certain colors because demons were attracted to them, or the color meant something (purple meant immorality, for instance). Even if I didn't wear the color, if someone around me did, it meant I was playing the harlot and going after other gods. It meant big trouble for me; God might even kill me.

I remember having a panic attack on a bus on my way to work. I prayed against as many demons as I could and asked forgiveness, all because someone near me had on a purple shirt.

My new clothes included blues, grays, and black. I hoped my husband would be happy with that. I figured he would, as a prophet of God.

I had a strong desire to relocate to California, the state of my birth. I'd just graduated from college, and it was the perfect time to go. After the intensive weeks of training by Seth, my family no longer appeared spiritual enough for me.

I was on to something big. My aunt validated my decision to marry Phil when she said she'd met him before and prayed with him. She described him as a true prayer warrior.

Seth allowed both my mother and my aunt to know who I was marrying and to follow me out to California for the wedding. I believe he arranged this so I would feel more secure and wouldn't suspect that this was a cultic thing, since my family members were present.

My first meeting with Phil at the motel brought disappointment. He was nothing like I expected. Taller than me, skinny, I found him kind of goofy. Knowing this was not a pure spiritual reaction to

God's choice for me, I put it down to nerves. Seth arranged that Phil and I would meet at the exact motel Phil dreamed about. Rhoda and I stayed in the room while Seth went to pick up Phil. My nervousness verged on downright fright. Rhoda recognized my fear and rebuked me. She insisted my weakness had allowed demons in.

■ My nervousness verged on downright fright. ■

We stayed in hotels for two weeks before our marriage while Seth looked for a place for us to live. Phil and I weren't allowed to be alone. Seth and Rhoda listened to all our conversations. The four of us prayed together to rebuke demons and went everywhere together. Seth and Phil constantly competed. If Phil did something better than Seth, Seth deemed it was demonic and said Phil was stealing his personality. I thought it childish. It also showed me Phil did not know as much about the spirit realm as Seth, and fear grew within me regarding marrying him. While Seth had all the answers, I would be stuck in California with someone unable to take care of all the demons. I was petrified.

Phil and I had nothing in common. If we had met in any other situation, we would never have been friends—perhaps not even acquaintances. We were polar opposites, and not in a nice, complementary way. Yet Seth said if I didn't marry Phil, I would be going against God's will, that He would be very angry with me, and I might lose my place in eternity. Since I thought I'd heard God say I was to marry Phil, too, I ignored my feelings.

As Seth married us, with an actual minister present to make it official, I couldn't believe I said the vows. I hoped all the rebukes for my lack of diligence and yelling about my inability to do anything right would stop once the wedding was over. Much later, Seth said I played the harlot when I married Phil, because in my heart I actually said my vows to him, because I desired him. How pompous! I didn't desire or marry either of them in my heart. I did what I had to because I feared dying by the hand of the Almighty.

The day after the wedding, everyone left. We were alone and on our own. Since we had no transportation, the delivery truck bringing our furniture came to the motel and picked us up. It felt like we were just pieces of furniture.

Seth had terrible taste. My credit card brought ugly furniture into our apartment, and I had no say in it. I'd always hated floral prints but discovered I now had a flowery couch of my own. The apartment consisted of a bedroom and a living room/kitchen. Fleas infested it, water leaked in, and the walls were thin. I hated being stuck someplace unfamiliar, with someone I didn't know, and no vehicle to go anywhere. The walk to the bus stop was long, too. Adding to the misery, Seth called daily, sometimes multiple times a day, and calls could last eight hours or more. His continuous yelling at me drove home the point of my inferiority, my "desire" for him (not Phil), and my horrible black heart that caused him so much trouble. He said demons attacked him continually because of me. Phil experienced attacks—also my fault. I wanted to die.

■ I wanted to die. ■

During one call, Seth told me my sister, Jennifer, had fully joined with the ministry, and she had incredible faith. His tone indicated I did not have great faith. He used his frequent calls to plant seeds of contention and strife between my sister and me. He knew I had always felt inferior to her, and he used it against me.

The next six years dragged by in a monotony of mental, physical, spiritual, emotional, and sexual abuse for me. Our lives were awful in every way. We had no friends, no family nearby, no car, no money. Anything bad that happened was my fault.

A year and a half later, I gave birth to our daughter, Ginny. Her birth should have been a wonderful time. Phil accompanied me for the delivery, but then left and didn't return until my release from the hospital. No baby shower, no gifts, no decorated nursery welcomed our wonderful daughter. We weren't allowed to bond as a family. Seth insisted that having a child reflected God's judgment on us. He forbade us to take her to the park, play with her, or do other normal things because she was God's child, and those activities were too worldly. If she cried or fussed, my demons caused it.

Six months after Ginny's birth, Phil stopped working. He forced me to earn our living. I worked up to four waitress jobs at a time, 60-80 hours a week. After my shifts, I took the bus home, cooked, cleaned, took care of Ginny, fought with demons through prayer, endured berating and sometimes abuse. I slept from one to three hours a night.

Phil slept all day, gave Ginny minimal care while I was away, didn't do any chores, and spent his day trying to come up with a list of which demons I'd let into my heart, so he could rebuke me when I got home.

■ If she cried or fussed, my demons caused it. ■

All the prophecies of glorious ministry work fell in tatters. We never did anything along those lines. I prayed with someone once at work, but Seth said not to do it again because our hearts were too black, and God couldn't use us to help anyone yet. Seth wasn't content with phone calls; he made us get a fax machine so he could fax demon names (to be cast out with prayer) and judgments from God. I hated that fax machine! The ever-present calls and faxes depressed me beyond words.

Seth and Rhoda came to visit us once. They said Seth received a word I would die and go to heaven soon, so they'd come to bury me. The good news? After death, I would be taught all the demon/spiritual warfare stuff I'd been too stupid to get a grip on while I was alive. After I died, Seth would raise me from the dead and then his ministry would come into full force. He said I had cancer, but I was actually pregnant with what turned out to be the first of two miscarriages. They stayed a month and I didn't die, so they left.

Despite the obvious difficulties of transportation and money, why didn't I take Ginny and leave? Things Seth did and said never completely added up or made sense, but he had a knack for drawing me in.

For example, once a wave of depression, fear, and loneliness swept over me. Shortly afterward, the phone rang and Seth said God told him to call because depression and fear had attacked me. He prayed about the demons, and I felt so much better. This happened several times. It seemed as though he could read my thoughts.

Even if what he described about me wasn't correct, he said he knew best because I wasn't connected to the Holy Spirit well enough to know my own heart and mind. Objecting meant going against God's prophet, which put me in line for a major punishment or hell itself. The few times he called it accurately convinced me of his power.

When our break from Seth's influence came, it surprised me. After a normal day of long shifts as a waitress, I arrived home, went to the bedroom, and took off all my clothes. I stripped because Phil said I was not to try to hide my sin under my clothes. I started to tell Phil all the sinful thoughts I'd had that day. In the midst of my list of sins, Phil asked if I liked Seth and being in the ministry. I said I did not. We talked about how neither of us liked Seth.

Phil said, "We're not going to talk to him anymore."

So we didn't.

I freaked out for a while, because I feared we would all go to hell, that demons had persuaded us to leave the prophet of God, but Phil reassured me. I began to hope things would change. Perhaps now, since Seth had ordered Phil not to get a job, he would get one. He didn't. I still bore the burden of working, cooking, cleaning, and taking care of Ginny. The rebukes didn't stop, nor did the sexual, mental, and emotional abuse. But at least he didn't beat me anymore.

■ I began to hope things would change. ■.

Once we broke from Seth, Phil decided to have his own ministry. It seemed like a good idea; we would help others get out of cults. We had dreams of being rich, of God dropping stuff from the sky, and Phil getting music and sports endorsements. Of course, none of that happened. We didn't go to church, get counseling, pay off our debts, or do any of the things we really needed to do. Phil said God didn't want us to do those things. I'd traded Seth's control for Phil's domination.

After twelve years of abuse and marriage, I left Phil and took Ginny with me. We moved to be near my sister, mom, and other relatives. In making this final break, God has been merciful. He helped me get a job, a car, a place to live (with my mom), restored friendships and family relationships, and so much more.

God is also healing me spiritually and emotionally. I have problems reading certain passages of the Bible, doing some things, going particular places, but every day it gets better. I went to the same counselors Jennifer and my mom went to. I feared telling them everything, but doing so brought healing. I also received counseling from a woman at church, as well as attending church, reading the Bible, worshipping, and pouring out my feelings in a journal. The healing process is different for everyone. Though I still struggle, I have come a long way. My fear, lack of trust, and emotional storms have given way to more peace as God gives me a grip on those things.

My main concern today is how this experience with the cult and abuse will impact Ginny. I cringe when I contemplate how it might all come to a head when she hits the teen years. She grew up without friends and always had to stay at home for fear demons would attack her. I home-schooled her, though I was unqualified to take on the task. I bought books wherever I could find some, whenever money would allow. Phil said she only needed to know about demons and God. When she got old enough, he put her to work making his meals when I was not home to do it.

Many things changed for Ginny when we rejoined my family. She began attending a Christian school. Initially, she had to be put back a year to help her catch up on basics. But after a year, she'd done so well she skipped a grade, and continues doing exceptionally well. My daughter has questions and concerns about what we went through, of course, and sees a counselor once a week. God is very good to her. Ginny has lots of friends, though sometimes she has trouble relating to kids her age. Her preferred friends are younger children or adults. Over time, our relationship is getting better. Phil continually put me down in front of her, said I was a bad mother and criticized me, so Ginny and I became somewhat disconnected. God is healing that, too.

■ My daughter has questions and concerns about what we went through. ■

I would like to find some sort of job or career in psychology, since that's what my degree is in. I want to help others. Having been married in a cult and raised my daughter to be that way, I have much empathy for other women in the same situation. I can also speak knowledgably to the issue of spousal abuse. I keep asking God to show me how to put what I've learned to good use.

Both in the cult and when I was with Phil, I wasn't allowed to like things or do what I wanted. Trying to figure out what I like is a bit overwhelming, but I'm taking little steps all the time. I took a course so I could get my motorcycle license, and it was a great experience. I pressed past the instilled terror of trying something I wanted to do without someone's approval, and am so glad I did.

Mind control is a serious matter. Despite a degree in psychology, having gone to church when I was young, even attending Christian schools, the cult sucked me in. Low self-esteem, a troubled childhood, rebellion, lack of stability in my life, a bad relationship with my father—any of these could be blamed. But I certainly didn't help the situation by making one bad choice after another. I believe the main reason for my vulnerability was the lack of a true relationship with Jesus and solid biblical knowledge. Had I dug a little deeper, I'm sure the truth would have been revealed. As I think it over today, I can see that it was, many times over; I just didn't know how to listen.

In this long and trying experience, God stayed with me, and He always will. If you are reading this and you've been (or are) in a cult, a bad marriage, been abused, are a single parent, spiritually confused, or are lonely and suicidal, take heart. God loves you. He can take anything and turn it around if we give Him the opportunity. He has turned my mourning to dancing (Psalm 30:11) and given me beauty for ashes (Isaiah 61:3).

Since the first publication of this book there have been many changes in my life. I am remarried to an amazing man, and have three stepsons. My husband was actually my childhood crush, whom I remet at work. The way God orchestrated our meeting again is a story all on its own. GInny made it through her teen years better than I ever would have imagined. Counseling, prayers, and God's miracles, we made it through, and continue to.

Marian's Story—A Mother's Heart

Every mother longs to become a friend to her daughters when they grow up. She gives birth to them, nurtures them, protects them as best she can, and finally releases them to fly on their own. I hoped the same for my relationship with my daughters as they entered their twenties. I knew our bumpy life in their childhood could have repercussions, and felt encouraged when I saw them begin to turn to God as young women.

My own spiritual journey had stalled for a time. I worshipped at an unchallenging church, and my second marriage had careened out of control. I longed for something more. When my sister told me about a man and his wife who seemed so close to God, I was intrigued. She said God spoke to them, gave him visions, and that he could discern the meaning of dreams and give prophecies over people. I had nothing to lose by meeting them—or so I thought.

From the first moment, I felt uncomfortable with Seth's eyes. They seemed to look right through me. He also didn't treat his wife very lovingly. I put this down to the fact that she seemed rebellious, not submissive, as I believed a pastor's wife should be. They made a strange pair but exuded friendliness and made me feel important. I craved that sensation. For the first time in a long time, I felt close to a pastor and his wife. It felt great.

Seth took an immediate liking to my younger daughter, Janice. He said she would be great in God's kingdom. I knew she'd been praying earnestly for direction and had rededicated her life to the Lord after a time of wandering. It elated me to think God planned to use her in a big way. My girls meant everything to me. I wanted the best for them. I couldn't have asked for anything more wonderful than God wanting Janice to be in His service.

Enthusiasm swept me along when my sister told me Seth had prophesied Janice would be like Rebekah in the Bible. He even began calling her by that name. Janice herself concurred. When he said she would go away and marry a man God had chosen for her, I had mixed feelings.

"Don't tell your husband or anyone else about this," Seth admonished. "They won't understand. Just say she's going to California to be part of a mission."

■ When he said she would go away and marry a man God had chosen for her, I had mixed feelings. ■

"But how can that be right? God wants honesty," I protested.

Seth looked into my eyes and smiled gently. "Don't worry. God knows what He's doing. And remember, He often had His servants tell half-truths when it served His purpose, like when Abraham said Sarah was his sister instead of his wife. She was his half sister, so it wasn't really a lie. Rebekah will go to California to be part of the ministry there. It's not a lie."

I didn't like it when she moved in with Seth and Rhoda until she was ready to go to California. All our conversations took place in Seth's presence from then on. When I doubted, he always had a Scripture handy or a "revelation" from God to persuade me again.

Janice and I did have a few minutes alone when she came home to pick up some clothes.

"Do you think I'm doing the right thing?" Afternoon sun slanted through the window and lit up the small pile of clothing as she packed.

"You said God told you to do it. Is that true?"

"Well, I did get a Scripture reference in my head when I was praying, and it was about Rebekah and Isaac."

"I can't say for sure if it is of the Lord, but it has to be better than us choosing husbands. Look at my two failed marriages."

I still wonder what would have happened if I'd tried to convince her otherwise.

My own world fell apart around the same time she left for the other side of the country. Seth said he'd had revelations about my husband, and I must leave him. My head spun. I didn't know what to believe, but I wanted to please God more than anything, so I moved out of the house and into the one my sister and her husband owned. This made things quite convenient for Seth, since it meant my husband would not ask questions about Janice when she moved away.

Life went into fast-forward. Janice made preparations to leave, and suddenly Jen got involved with Seth and Rhoda. A few weeks later, she, too, was told to divorce her husband and sell everything she had. This made me very uncomfortable. How can this be of God? Why would He have Jen get a divorce? She has no grounds for it. I kept asking God for answers, but Jen assured me she was fine with it. Seth had told her that her husband had been unfaithful.

During her initial time in the group, Seth kept Jennifer's whereabouts secret from me. He brought her to our house on a few occasions but never left the room so I could talk to her alone. She said Seth and Rhoda had become her spiritual parents and began to address me as "Marian." I discovered they'd moved her to her own little house, and she'd quit her job. I couldn't understand why or how they were supporting her. The few questions I could ask her drew tired sighs and wan smiles.

"Things are hard. But I wouldn't have it any other way. I'm learning to be a servant of God."

I wanted to believe everything was all right and that Seth taught correct doctrine. After all, didn't the Bible say that if we loved family more than we loved Him, we were not worthy of Him? Everything seemed to come down to submission. I didn't dare question God or His servant, Seth.

Besides, if I did so, I would no longer have contact with Jen. I'd already lost contact with Janice; all correspondence between us had to go through Seth's hands. I only got cards from her on Christmas and Easter. Both my girls concerned me, and Jen in particular, but she assured me everything was fine, she claimed to be learning so much and said they loved her.

■ Everything seemed to come down to submission. I didn't dare question God or His servant, Seth. ■

I'm not good at rocking the boat, and I hate to hurt people's feelings. Seth ordered me to move out of my sister's house and in with Jen. I hated the way it happened. He said I had to move out while they were on vacation and leave a note. I will never forget how that hurt my sister. Once in the new house, Jen took charge of me. Seth pitted us against each other constantly. I saw so much fear in Jen. She had changed. We weren't allowed to talk to each other except when Jen corrected me and scolded me. She even struck me once. That hurt emotionally more than physically, but I knew in my heart she didn't mean it.

She did what she had to do to survive. The days were long and hard, working 50-60 hours a week, plus constantly trying to determine the real intentions of our hearts so they could be corrected.

I realized how frightened Jen had become when I watched Seth hollering at her the first time. I knew in my heart he must be hitting her, too. I cried inside. I could hardly stand it, but there appeared to be no way out. We had cut ourselves off from everyone out of fear. Seth brainwashed us into thinking the way we lived was God's will for our lives and that our progress displeased Him terribly. The way to please God: work harder and give more money. I wanted to leave many times but knew if I did, I'd never see my girls again. Jen became convinced she'd go to hell if she left. In time, I believed the same lie.

■ I wanted to leave many times, but knew if I did, I'd never see my girls again. ■

Another move brought us to a smaller house. Because of our closer proximity, my eyes opened to the physical and mental abuse Jen endured. It broke my heart. Seth made her gain a tremendous amount of weight and work double shifts as a waitress each day. My heart went out to her. She had a punishing physical routine serving tables from 5:30 a.m. until 9:00 or later at night. Once she arrived home, the phone calls began. Hours on end of drilling and berating her left her a zombie. The routine was insane. Why, God? Why do You want her treated like this? It made no sense to me.

The night Seth pounded Jen with a metal slotted spoon in the kitchen, he ordered me to my room. I begged God to stop it. I knew it couldn't be from Him. God was supposed to be loving. Where was the love?

I finally suspected Seth of abusing Jen sexually and confronted him.

"That question came right out of your own heart." He pointed at my chest. "You are hoping I'll fall in love with your daughter and get rid of Rhoda. You think Rhoda doesn't deserve me, but Jennifer does."

His ability to turn every question back on us stunned me. The answer, he said, was to give more money to the Lord to cleanse my mind. Each demand for money meant increased hardship for us. The only cash we had came from waitressing. In order to pay our living expenses, after we gave Seth what he demanded from our funds, we pulled out the credit cards.

I mentally blocked out the subject of Seth and Jen again until one day he came over and asked for more money. As he moved to the door, he stopped. "Your daughter is evil in the sight of God. I had no idea how evil, but God showed me. She won't stop lusting after me, so God got her pregnant as a punishment. Then He made me force her to have an abortion. God absolutely hates her."

I nearly doubled over in anguish at his words. All Jen ever wanted was to be married and have children. This man had robbed her of both. God did not do this! My stomach heaved, and I felt light-headed. I didn't say a word, and Seth left. Grief consumed me. This man is insane. We have to get out of here before he kills her. I dropped to my knees and begged God to help us.

I also prayed for Jen's safety on her day off each week.

The fear that I'd come home to an empty house gripped me. Seth threatened repeatedly to kill her, cut her up in little pieces, and dispose of her. He said no one would miss her. I knew if she were not home when I got there, I would call the police. I didn't care if I went to hell for it. I had to save Jen.

The revelation about the abortion represented the final turning point. A short time later I broke my arm and couldn't work as a waitress. With our income cut in half, Seth made Jen sell her car to raise more money. When I started back to work, we shared my car—and discovered we finally had a place to talk without him finding out. We even took the long way home but feared to go further. Jennifer said she wanted to leave, but fear kept her captive. Terror held us both in place for a time, but God's grace kept bringing things to show us we needed to leave, and that He did love us. We wouldn't go to hell if we left. But if we stayed, we were certainly both headed for death.

◼ Terror held us both in place. ◼

I regret so much of what happened in the ten years we lived under Seth's thumb, but one thing I will always treasure: I now know God loves us and never forsakes us. We did horrid things toward each other and toward Him. Seth forced us to tell God we hated Him, to swear at and curse God, even to bind the Holy Spirit and rip Him out of ourselves. I can remember saying the words, but pleading in my heart for Him to not leave me.

Through all of this, God never abandoned or gave up loving us. He truly is love. If you are in a church that has no love, it has no God. If you are told to separate yourself from other believers and family members, RUN. Never allow your pastor to become your idol or your parental figure. It only opens a door for deception. Go back to the Word-study the Bible—to make sure what you're being taught is not out of context. Follow Jesus daily, and let Him direct your paths. Think for yourself; God gave you intelligence.

Fight for your spiritual life.

◼ Thinking It Through ◼

Your Family or Your Soul

Cult membership is difficult to walk away from in the best circumstances. When family members are also involved in the same group, the choices can seem impossible. A person leaving the cult is instantly shunned by everyone else in the group, particularly biological family members. For many, this prospect is daunting enough to keep them in bondage for years.

Jennifer and her mother, though forbidden to speak to each other even when living under the same roof, drew strength from each other. The threat of never seeing each other again frightened them both. Seth added pressure by saying anyone who left would spend eternity in hell, and any contact with that person would doom others to the same fate. With the future of one's soul supposedly on the line, if family members are also entrapped, it is no wonder many stay in cults long after they would have normally left.

Janice and her family left Seth's control sooner than other family members. It was somewhat easier for them to cut themselves off from Seth by not answering the telephone and unplugging the fax machine. However, since the family didn't break with Seth's ideas and theology (just his immediate interaction) they were as captive when "free" as they had been in the group. Until Janice and Ginny physically left their home and began to clear their heads and hearts of the poison of deception, they were doomed to repeat the behaviors that held them prisoner.

The brave family members who exit a cult and leave loved ones behind do so by embracing specific truths that give them strength and courage.

TRUTH: The cult leader has no control over your soul's destiny.

He or she can't curse you to eternal hell, yank you from God's hand if you belong to Him, or send demons after you to torment you for the rest of your life. The cult leader is a human being, limited by time, space, and finite human frailty. Only God has the power to save or condemn. His desire is to see everyone saved. Let go of the cult leader's hand and embrace Jesus by believing in His complete payment for all your sins (past, present, and future) by His sacrificial death on the cross and His resurrection to new life. Trust in His ability to keep you safe. "For I am persuaded, that neither death, nor life, nor angels, nor principalities, nor powers, nor things present, nor things to come, nor height, nor depth, nor any other created thing, will be able to separate us from the love of God, which is in Christ Jesus our Lord" (Romans 8:38-39).

TRUTH: You have no power to condemn anyone else.

You may have been told that simply trying to contact family members who remain in the group will cause them to spend eternity in torment. God gave you a good mind, if you'll just plug back in to it. You are a finite person, with individual actions for which you are responsible. That is the extent of your power. You must choose your own path. Others have the same options, and cannot be condemned by what you do. Every person is individually answerable to God—and no one else, when it comes to his or her soul. "For we must all appear before the judgment seat of Christ, that each one may receive the things done in the body, according to that he has done, whether good or bad" (2 Corinthians 5:10, NKJV).

TRUTH: You have been lied to intentionally.

A preacher or pastor can get off track and say something that is not biblical. However, if he is truly a man of God, he'll be corrected by the Holy Spirit and will repent of what he's said. He'll admit it to his congregation and return the people to an accurate understanding of Scripture. Someone who gets off track, ignores the true meaning of the Bible, and uses its verses to subdue, imprison, and control other believers, is doing so consciously. If you are in (or have been in) a cult, this has happened to you.

God has strong negative feelings about such deception. In Jeremiah 23 a situation arose in which those who were supposed to lead Israel and nurture the people spiritually were doing the opposite. Jeremiah wrote, "Thus saith the Lord of hosts, 'Hearken not unto the words of the prophets that prophesy unto you: they make you vain: they speak a vision of their own heart, and not out of the mouth of the Lord… I have not sent these prophets, yet they ran: I have not spoken to them, yet they prophesied. But if they had stood in my counsel, and had caused my people to hear my words, then they should have turned them from their evil way, and from the evil of their doings'" (verses 16, 21–22, KJV).

If your leader's teachings do not align with the Bible both in word and in the spirit in which they were intended, back away. Find better instruction.

TRUTH: Opposite "truths" can't both be true.

Cult teachings don't hold up when compared with what the Bible says. If a leader tells you God hates you and hopes you go to hell, take courage: that's not what the Bible teaches. "Behold, what manner of love the Father hath bestowed upon us, that we should be called the sons of God" (1 John 3:1, KJV). If he or she extends salvation one day and pulls it back the next, fear not: the Bible says just the opposite. "These things I have written unto you that believe in the name of the Son of God; that ye may know that ye have eternal life, and that ye may believe on the name of the Son of God" (1 John 5:13, KJV). It is our responsibility to use our minds and hearts to put teachers to the test. If they don't coincide with truth, they are to be avoided. "Beloved, believe not every spirit, but try the spirits whether they are of God: because many false prophets are gone out into the world" (1 John 4:1, KJV).

TRUTH: Scripture can be twisted to mean whatever a leader wants it to.

The Bible can be a blessing or an instrument of torture, depending on the hands in which it is held. False teachers find weapons in the Bible by taking verses out of context or reinterpreting them for their own benefit. When a follower objects, the very words are pointed to in the Bible, silencing dissent. Recognizing this danger is the first step in reforging the Bible into the weapon it is intended to be—the sword of the Spirit of God.

If you have been beaten with verses and whipped with biblical phrases, you can reclaim the truth of Scripture by reading the verses for yourself, in their full context. Do not be surprised if it takes awhile for you to relax in reading the Bible again. Your deceiver electrified the Word so just a touch would injure you. Gradually you will stop hearing his or her voice when you delve into the riches of the Bible, and God can speak His truth to you again. It takes work, but the effort is worthwhile. "Study to shew thyself approved unto God, a workman that needeth not to be ashamed, rightly dividing the word of truth" (2 Timothy 2:15, KJV).

TRUTH: Life outside the cult is not a "lesser" life.

A prime lie of cultic leaders is that the only people living righteously, having spiritual peace and enjoying God's favor are inside their group. Unfortunately, they don't have to go farther than the newspaper or television headlines to point out corruption, sin, and moral collapse in our society. We live in a fallen, sinful world, and have since Adam and Eve sinned in the Garden of Eden. Despite these problems, not everyone outside the cult is bound for hell. There are many godly people who follow the teachings of Christ, worship God with their whole heart and enjoy peace. The teachings of cult leaders are not higher wisdom; they are wrong. God freely offers a life of spiritual fulfillment, not to those who follow a particular person's teachings, but the teaching of Jesus. "I am come that they might have life, and that they might have it more abundantly. I am the good shepherd: the good shepherd giveth his life for the sheep" (John 10:10-11, KJV).

TRUTH: You can have peace with God.

You were not created to live in continual fear. God wants so much more for you. "For God hath not given us the spirit of fear; but of power, and of love, and of a sound mind" (2 Timothy 1:7, KJV). If you awake each day and fear descends on your heart lest you step out of line, or you feel oppressed instead of invigorated when you think of God, it's time to reconsider what you're being taught. "Be careful [anxious] for nothing; but in every thing by prayer and supplication with thanksgiving let your requests be made known unto God. And the peace of God, which passeth all understanding, shall keep your hearts and minds through Christ Jesus" (Philippians 4:6-7, KJV).

Leaving a cult or spiritually abusive group is wrenching; leaving family members behind is even worse. But the only way you can hope to help them is to get help and heal spiritually, yourself. It is entirely possible you will have to leave alone. Remember, you are not responsible for their reaction to you leaving the group, any more than you can direct their eternal destiny. Do what you must to recover from the deceptive path you've gone down. Ask God to lead them to freedom when they are ready, and be there to help when they need it.

Chapter 8

The Searching Heart

The fire pulses with a soothing orange glow, flames streaming up the sides of logs. Occasional pops send showers of bright sparks skyward to momentarily mimic the shining stars in the clear night sky. A soft breeze blows around the group at the fire, just enough to keep them on their log seats, hands extended into the intimate warmth.

A bag of marshmallows makes the rounds again, and sticky branches are extended into the glowing coals. The smell of warm sugar settles low to the ground, enveloping them in contentment.

In the distance, other campfires flicker through the trees. Gary shifts his weight to find the perfect spot to brown the marshmallow on his stick. "We love camping with you guys." He smiles at his lifelong friends Bill and Kim, and the new couple, Krystal and Jim, across the flames.

"The more the merrier," Krystal says, then turns to blow out the flames on her now-blackened treat. "I have lots of fond memories of camping when I was a kid." Her gaze dances across Gary's kids and her own family who had joined together for the weekend.

"Who's got the graham crackers?" one of the others asks, and the box begins its stop-and-go circle around the popping logs.

"You seem awful quiet this weekend." Krystal catches the crispy black marshmallow between graham cracker and chocolate bar, slides it off the stick, and tosses the twig into the flames.

Gary's smile dips on one side as he contemplates the fire. "Sorry. Sometimes I replay everything in my head, wondering how my life turned out this way. I know eventually it will straighten out again. I have to trust God on that, but for now it feels like a whirlpool I can't quite swim out of. The divorce really took the wind out of my sails."

The man to Gary's left sighs and knocks some mud out of the treads of his hiking boots with a bent tent stake he'd found on the ground and nods in commiseration.

Gary tosses his marshmallowy stick into the fire. "My credit's a mess, my kids are confused and angry, my life blew up, and I don't think I've hit ground yet after being blown sky high. When I do, I know it's gonna hurt."

Krystal shakes her head. "You're such a nice guy. You should be mobbed by women looking for somebody like you."

Gary chuckles. "Thanks, but that's not exactly been my history. I've prayed to God for the right wife, knowing He is perfectly capable of bringing her into my life, but so far He's keeping her under wraps. For all I know, I've already met her, but I'm not aware of it. I guess for now I need to keep my head down and get myself back on track…let God take care of the future."

"Still, I wish I could think of someone for you…" She munches thoughtfully on the last of her S'more.

* * *

Krystal can hardly dial the numbers fast enough. When the phone is picked up at the other end of the line, she doesn't wait for the greeting.

"You're never going to believe who just called me!"

"I could start guessing, but there are over six billion people on the planet…" Marcie's exasperation makes Krystal smile.

"My ex-sister-in-law!"

Silence.

"Jennifer—the one who joined a cult and divorced my husband's brother. Remember?"

"You told me about that. Wasn't that a long time ago? What's she doing calling now?"

"It was almost ten years ago. She and her mother just got out of that group they were in. They've been in it all this time!"

"Wow. That's pretty creepy. What did she say?"

"She sounded really scared at the beginning. But she called to ask forgiveness for ignoring my advice to stay away from the group and stick with John. I really tried to stop her, but she was pretty strong-headed."

"Did you forgive her? I think I'd have hung up."

"Marcie! It takes a lot of guts to admit to someone you made a huge mistake and ask for forgiveness. Of course I gave it to her. I'm thrilled to hear she's out. She and I were really close back then. Even after she and John started having problems, I was more worried about losing a friend than losing a sister-in-law."

"Did she sound like a weirdo?"

"She sounded pretty great, actually, once we got over the initial part of the conversation. I'm so happy for her. She asked about John, and I told her he's remarried. She wants to talk to him, too."

"What good will that do? Is she trying to get him back? Too late for that!"

"No, she just wants to apologize to him, too. I know he was so worried about her when she joined that thing, and he'll be glad to know she's out at last. It feels like I spoke to someone who rose from the grave. I never thought I'd hear from her again."

"Did she give you all the gory details?"

"No, and I didn't ask. That's up to her to share when she's ready. But it renews my faith in God eventually straightening things out for people."

* * *

The telephone is still an instrument of momentary terror for me in the first weeks after leaving the cult. I associate it with Seth's late-night berating calls. I know it's going to take some time for me to again think of it as bringing someone into my life that I actually want to hear from.

I pick it up gingerly, out of habit.

"Jen! It's Krystal. How are you?"

"Hey, Krystal. I'm doing well. Getting ready for my shift at the diner in an hour or so. What's up?"

"I heard from John that you guys had a really good conversation. I'm so glad. I'm calling because I can't get you out of my head. I know a guy who would be perfect for you!"

I sink into a chair and groan. "What are you talking about?

I just got out of a cult. My mind and emotions are scrambled, I'm fifty pounds overweight. I don't even know what direction is up. No way do I want to get involved with someone."

"But, Jen, he's perfect! A great Christian guy, with a sweet heart and really a deep spiritual person."

"I appreciate what you're trying to do, but I'm not ready for that kind of thing. I may never be…"

* * *

Cinderella and the slipper

THE LAST THING ON MY MIND after getting out of the cult was a boyfriend. Yet it seemed to be the first thing on the minds of friends when they learned I'd broken free. I turned down all their suggestions.

I'd just spent ten years under the control of a man who had anything but my best interests at heart. Deeply wounded by that relationship, I had spent a decade not practicing the basic things women do to attract men. I felt like an inept teenager.

When Seth broke off our intimate relationship, he turned on me viciously and demanded that I put on fifty pounds as fast as I could. Complying had been easier than undergoing his abuse. My first days of freedom found me overweight, with self-esteem that would look up to a mushroom. And friends wanted me to meet these "perfect men" they kept mentioning? It was out of the question.

My ex-sister-in-law was not the only one. A coworker said she had a cousin who wanted to meet me. She said he knew all about me being in a cult, and that didn't bother him. He'd been in the restaurant and seen me and asked her for my story. "If he asks you out, you should go," she urged. "He's a Christian, and he'd make a nice friend to have right now. His name's Gary."

The way I felt about my body, my emotional stability, and my uncertain future made the likelihood of great men lining up to meet me completely unreal. I dodged their match-making attempts and went about the early stages of my healing process. I focused on working with Grace and Ira. Everything else could come later. Much later.

It seemed as though I was waving a red flag at bulls, though. Krystal in particular would not let up.

"Aren't you the least bit curious? This guy already knows about you. He's a customer at the diner, and he's seen you there. He still wants to meet you. Are you sure you're not interested?"

One day as she pushed me yet again, a light bulb went on in my mind. "Wait a minute, Krystal. This guy's name isn't Gary, is it?"

"Yes! How did you know?"

Not a line of men at my door…one man with a line of promoters.

* * *

A handsome, dark-haired man showed up at the diner counter that night. "I think we have some mutual friends," he said. "I'm Gary Redcay."

"I'm glad you came in tonight," I blurted. "If you'd waited a week, I would have been so nervous."

■ A handsome, dark-haired man showed up at the diner counter that night. ■

The discomfort inherent in meeting each other dissolved in the face of honesty and laughter. Since I now worked as the assistant manager and hostess at the diner, I could stand at the counter and talk to Gary when I was not leading people to their tables or working the register. For me, it was an ideal situation. When things got scary, I could move away, knowing he'd be there when I returned.

We had great conversations over the ensuing weeks. Gary came in every night and drank pots of coffee. He told me his story. I told him the parts of my story I felt comfortable sharing at that time. We focused on becoming friends, nothing more. Though I shared some of my experiences in the cult, I could tell he didn't really understand.

He doesn't get it. He doesn't understand the trauma I went through, or the whole spiritual warfare thing. And I haven't told him everything…

Gary wasn't what I'd call "my type," but the more we talked and got acquainted, I found myself becoming attracted to him. He was so nice, I couldn't help it.

We talked about our lives, our likes and dislikes, shared jokes. One night I mentioned that I wanted to buy the movie Facing the Giants. A few days later he came in with one of his daughters and handed me a small package.

"It's a Christmas present."

Inside I found the movie, but the tag made me smile even more: To Jennifer, from the Redcays, it read. Not from him, but the whole family. It was a cute way to make me feel included.

We'd been out of the cult only a few months, and Christmas was coming up fast.

"What are your plans for Christmas?" Gary asked one night as coffee steamed in front of him.

"Oh, we're not doing anything." I laughed. "We don't even have money for a tree. And after ten years of not having Christmas, the whole thing is a little overwhelming for us."

He nodded and took a sip of coffee. I thought that would be the end of it.

A week later, Mom and I got off shift and went home. On the porch we found a small live Christmas tree, completely decorated with lights and shiny balls, and a large poinsettia sitting next to it. The card said, From Gary and Krystal, who I later learned had helped him shop for it.

My heart melted like winter snow in spring.

This guy totally went out of his way for me. He didn't have to do that.

I looked up his number and called to thank him. "You have no idea what it meant to me."

"I couldn't imagine your first Christmas in ten years—you need to celebrate it."

We continued our cozy routine of chatting over coffee at the diner counter, but my view of him began to change.

How could it not?

A few days after he'd given me the Christmas tree, he suddenly stopped coming in. Three days went by, and I spent it arguing with myself. I fought liking him but woke up one morning knowing I'd fallen in love with him. It stunned me, scared me, exhilarated me.

■ I fought liking him but woke up one morning knowing I'd fallen in love with him. ■

I couldn't bring myself to call him, so I called Krystal and asked for an explanation. Match-maker that she is, she immediately called Gary and told him I was missing him. It was his first real glimmer of hope.

* * *

I'd told Grace, Ira and the counseling group about Gary. I worried that I might be taking the affections I'd had for one man and desperately settling them on the first person who treated me kindly. I also didn't want to put him before my relationship with the Lord. I'd already had experience in unhealthy relationships and didn't want another.

They assured me having a friend who came in every day could be very helpful to me. I took it as permission, of a kind.

Gary took me on a real date, not one of our "diner dates" at the counter in front of a restaurant of people. We went to a restaurant where I would not be waiting on people, but could enjoy being served myself for once. There was a forty-five minute waiting time for a table, so we went to run an errand and talked in the car.

Being alone together was a novel experience for us. Our diner dates had given us a certain intimacy as we'd shared about our lives, frustrations, dreams, and faith. We'd even begun sharing with each other what we'd like in a mate. Gary hinted that I might, in fact, be that person for him. I knew I had some tough things to share before I could ever trust his feelings. The quiet warmth of the idling car gave me courage.

■ I had some tough things to share before I could ever trust his feelings. ■

"I have to tell you some things about what happened to me these past few years, and I really don't want to do it. I don't know if you'll accept me when you know. But I want to be up front with you."

"I'd rather you tell me now. I know you've kept some things to yourself, but I want to know you—problems and all."

It was hard to get started, but once I did I couldn't stop. I told him everything. The physical and sexual abuse, the abortion, the mind control, the spiritually damaged condition I was in. When I finished, he looked out the windshield in silence into the night.

"If you want to take me home, that's OK. I understand. But I couldn't handle starting to date you and then a month later tell you all this and have you say you didn't want to see me again."

Rather than pushing Gary away, my story seemed not to faze him at all. Perhaps he'd guessed or even imagined it—or worse—when he wondered what I hadn't yet shared. I almost wondered why he didn't run away from me screaming. Instead, we had a wonderful dinner and continued our conversation at the house afterwards.

I was bubbling and floating when I went to counseling the following Friday full of the news and pleasure of the date. I didn't anticipate my counselors' reaction at all.

"Whoa! What are you saying? You went on a date? Oh, Jen, you're not ready for that!"

"A friend is one thing, but we don't think you should be dating yet. You've only begun to heal. So little time has passed since you've been out. Three months isn't long enough."

"You need to work through things before you dive into something this overwhelming. Take it slowly. We thought you were just having coffee at the diner with him. This is way too soon. You need to concentrate on getting well before you start dating someone. That's fair to you and him."

Their response devastated me. My trusted counselors said I'd taken a step in the wrong direction.

I called Gary in tears. "I feel so horrible! It's like a light went on in my darkness at last, and now they're telling me to turn it off, or at least close the door and ignore it for now. They said it would be best if we didn't talk on the phone or date, but just meet at the diner when I'm working." I sobbed and tried to blow my nose without blowing out his eardrum. "I know God gave me these counselors, and I should listen to them. But I want to spend time with you, too."

His answer shaped my reaction and my heart. "Jen, if this is from God for our lives, it's all right to wait. A month, a year, it won't matter. We'll each pray every day that if it's God's will, He'll confirm it for us, and if not, that He'll let us both know in our spirits. And I'll drink a lot more coffee at the diner."

* * *

The New Year came and I went to California with Mom for ten days to visit my dad. It was a wonderful, healing trip, but I missed seeing Gary every day. When I returned, we got back on track with diner dates, and Gary began to float on coffee again. I have no idea how he drank it all.

At the end of January, I went back to my counselors about the issue.

"I really, really want your blessing to date Gary. I went to California and dealt with issues about my dad and abandonment in my childhood, and I'm doing well."

"We've been praying about it, too, and we feel the same peace you do. We think you're ready now to move beyond friendship—but take it slow."

I called Gary, so excited I almost couldn't speak, and told him the news. He was elated.

"Ira and Grace want to meet you, too." I thought that would intimidate him; it did not.

"I want to meet them, too. I want to learn any way I can help you get better."

We had our first official date on February 3, 2008. Nine days later, Gary went to dinner with Ira and Grace. I was at work, my heart on pins and needles as I wondered what their discussion would be like.

I didn't have to wait long. Gary came into the diner after his meeting. I had time for a break, so we sat in the car to talk.

"It was wonderful. They're great, and they are so determined to help you past this damage in your life. I respect them."

"What did you talk about?"

"We talked about what you've been through and how it has affected you, what I can expect to be problems in the future, how to handle them."

I absorbed that phrase, the future.

"I told Ira I feel I am supposed to marry you. I asked him how he felt about that, and whether or not he thought you were ready. He said, 'The sooner, the better.'" Gary laughed. "The look on his face when he said it told me he hadn't expected to say that. God put those words in his mouth."

My head spun.

Gary reached for my hand and held it in both of his. "Jennifer, I love you. I've been praying for eight months for God's perfect will—not His permissive will, but His perfect will—for my life. I've asked Him to give me a clean slate, and prepare the heart of my wife. I've watched you and seen Him doing that. Jennifer, will you marry me?"

"Yes." It was the easiest word I'd ever said.

We discussed different dates for the wedding, and settled on April 11, just two months away. Excitement colored my world and reflected from the facets of the diamond in the ring we bought the next day at the mall.

* * *

Most women dream of their wedding day, even if it's a second marriage. As we moved toward our special day, I felt anxiety ripple through my every thought.

Where are we going to get married? How many people will be there? How will we afford it?

The first pastor we approached to do the service already had an overbooked wedding schedule at his church. In the end, we asked Ira and Grace if we could hold it at their home, a cozy old stone farmhouse with a great-room where their house church met. I wanted to limit the guests to forty-five people, and that's exactly how many chairs they had. Most of all, I wanted to avoid making a spectacle of myself coming down an aisle. Still uneasy being in public, the idea of a crowd paralyzed me.

On April 11, 2008 we stood together before friends and family for a half-hour ceremony binding our lives together. Our hearts had already been joined, and making it official was beautiful. The pastor chose the book of Job for his wedding message.

"God made the second half of Job's life better than the first. He'd lost everything, but God restored what the locusts had eaten. You've both been through trials and difficulties, but God is mending all that. It will be exciting to see Him restore you both. Hand-in-hand, I know the work will go easier."

It was the perfect ceremony and message for us.

Gary's Story

Our wedding day culminated a path that started with Jen's ex-sister-in-law and that evening around a campfire. When she called to tell me she'd thought of someone for me, I was surprised but interested. She gave me pictures of Jen from her first wedding, and a modeling photo from when she'd worked in that field for a brief time.

"Don't go see her; she's not ready yet," she warned me.

Of course, I couldn't resist. I went to the diner to try to figure out who she was, without approaching or bothering her. I'd been there before and even seen Jen. She'd looked lifeless, sad, deep, withdrawn, and burdened. She didn't look healthy. When I spotted her this time, the healing process had already begun. She talked more to her customers. She walked with a spring to her step. By the time I introduced myself, she'd started wearing makeup, doing her hair, dressing different, holding herself in a more confident way.

Today, she's gorgeous, caring, healthy, vibrant—the most beautiful thing in my life. She's still a work in progress as far as healing emotional scars, but if the external is any indication, that will come in time.

Seeing a woman at a diner night after night could have driven some men crazy, but it felt good to take it slow. My life had been so chaotic up to that point. We probably got to know each other better that way than if we'd gone out on real dates. All we could do was talk. No movie or dinner could distract us—we simply talked over lots and lots of coffee.

Our first date began on a somber note when she told me the ugliest side of her cult experience. The Holy Spirit must have been preparing me for what I would hear. I felt sadness for her, but I had no concern about whether we would be able to have a relationship. Not once did I think this was too much baggage for me to deal with, because I had been through a lot, as well. I've always believed that God is bigger than any situation. I also recognized God's hand; everything would be fine.

■ I've always believed that God is bigger than any situation. ■

On Ira and Grace's advice, we pulled back a bit after our first date. They provided valuable counsel for Jen at a time she really needed them.

Once we began dating officially, I went to see them with her for premarital counseling. They helped us with some things from my past, and we faced issues that might continue to be a problem for a while in our marriage because of Jen's experiences.

I realized she needed plenty of love and affection. I showed her that by holding her hand, giving her a kiss on the cheek, a hug. She needed lots of human touch; she'd not been hugged in ten years. For our first date after we received Ira and Grace's blessing, we just went on a trip to the mall, holding hands as we walked, and stopping at Olive Garden afterward for dessert—she loves their tiramisu.

As with any marriage, ours has rough spots we're working to polish down to smoothness. The time she spent in the cult developed in Jen a habit of dreaming vividly every night. She still does, and it keeps her from getting enough sleep. It makes me feel so bad when she doesn't get the rest she needs, and I wish she could shut off her mind and lose herself in sleep. The other part, to be blunt, is our physical relationship. Because of the sexual abuse she experienced, the hesitations or limitations it causes intrude sometimes. She's come a long way in this area, but we're still making the journey together.

What makes it all easier is that I know she loves me deeply. Even though we have so much in common, we also have strengths and weaknesses that complement each other. We dream of a day when we're debt-free, so we can give to others through whatever avenue God provides. Jen is now a stay-at-home mother and we hope she can share her story with those who are hurting.

Because I met Jen, I have a greater spiritual awareness and understanding of the spiritual realm. I also have a greater appreciation of God's favor and love for both of us, because He has restored our lives. As a result, God's given me a passion to take back ground the enemy has taken and help others take it back, too—especially people who are struggling in their marriages.

■ Because I met Jen, I have a great spiritual awareness and understanding of the spiritual realm. ■

Through understanding Jen's experience and learning more about spiritual warfare, I realize how much the enemy had rights and strongholds in my first marriage. I was a casual Christian and did not take my proper place as the spiritual leader of the household. Now I realize what I must do. Jen and I pray together every morning to start our day. This is something I did not do in my first marriage. I have become more of a prayer warrior and intercessor for my family and friends. It started before Jennifer but grew as I started praying for her. When I didn't know how to pray for her, God gave me words and taught me.

As our lives mend, God is blending them together into a finished work that gets better every day. God's favor has been so evident in our lives. Before I met Jennifer, I was "in the Lord's face." I had made a mess of my life, but was finally ready for God's perfect will for my life. I remember crying out to Him in my car while driving to work, asking Him to give me the wife He wanted for me—a woman who loved Him more than me.

I hope our story will help other people find healing, restoration, and favor like we have. It's all about submitting wholly to the Lordship of Jesus Christ and allowing Him to work in our lives. He is faithful; we've seen it.

■ Thinking It Through... ■

It's Not Over When It's Over

A boy falls from his bike and breaks his arm. The doctor puts on a cast and leaves it on for six weeks. When the cast comes off, the bone is mended…the arm looks fine, but it will take physical therapy to restore the lost muscle tone.

A woman has a gall bladder attack and is raced to the hospital. The organ is removed…but she is placed on a special diet for the rest of her life to prevent further problems.

A family's mini-van collides with a car driven by a careless driver at an intersection. Within moments the members of the family are lined up on the sidewalk, unharmed, examining the damage to the vehicle. Though a tow truck will be called, it will be weeks before dents are removed from the bodywork. and longer still before their nerves are restored when driving in traffic.

Leaving a cult, abusive relationship, or aberrant group does not solve all the problems. In fact, it may be just the beginning for many difficulties.

Jennifer and her mother walked out of the group they were in with not much more than the clothes on their backs. Though invisible, they carried deep emotional scars, spiritual confusion, social inhibitions, a credit rating in tatters, and the need for regenerative therapy in many areas of their lives. At the writing of this book, they have been recovering since October 2007, but the echoes of their experience still linger.

If you are leaving a cult (or you know someone who is) people around you will often have unreal expectations about how quickly you will recover. The emotional and lifestyle wrench you've been through should be compared to cancer, not the flu, in terms of recovery time and complexity.

Keep It Real

For the ex-cult member, the world outside the old group is probably noisy, intimidating, frightening, even dangerous. Keep some of the things Jennifer learned in mind.

Healing is a process, not an event.

Jennifer: "I had a lot of flashbacks in my early days out of the group. Ideas were pounded into me for ten years. They don't go away overnight. Marrying Gary brought both wonder and anxiety. So many of the prohibitions in the cult had to do with isolating myself from other people to keep demons from transferring between us. Suddenly, I lived in a house with someone who talked to me, touched me all the time, sat on the same furniture I did, and put his clothes in the same hamper as mine. We slept in the same bed and showered in the same bathroom. When it became overwhelming, I'd have a panic attack. But it has eased up in the years since then, and I know the truth. Prayer is the best way to push back."

People can help or hurt.

Jennifer: "My counselors did their best to shield me from hurt early in my recovery. They helped me refrain from getting involved with Gary until we were all sure he had my best interests in mind.

Many people come out of cults and get caught up by unscrupulous people who put them right back in bondage. It's a delicate time and must be walked gently."

Reconnect wisely.

Jennifer: "When Gary and I got married and started going to church together with his kids, I had some uncomfortable experiences in a Sunday school class. People are still human. They don't know what you've been through and may say things that hurt you without realizing it. I would talk about my beliefs, and people actually laughed at me. One Sunday morning the teacher went on and on about the "unforgivable" sin of abortion, and how it was wrong in any situation. While I agree with him that it is wrong, I didn't like his approach. My mind raced with rebuttals. You need to be careful. You have no idea who might be sitting in your class or listening, or what they went through before coming here. I agree with what you are saying, but you need to say it in a spirit of love and compassion. Someone might have been pushed to that point, but thank God, He forgives.

"After that, I said I would go to the church, but never the Sunday school class again. We eventually changed churches to one where we both felt comfortable with the worship and the people.

"We didn't attend church while in the cult. If we had, perhaps the truth would have set us free a lot sooner. The first Sunday I attended church after leaving the group, the worship leader opened his Bible and read Psalm 18. I burst into tears and had to sit down, weeping as he read. It was the same psalm I read just before we broke free, and it was God's way of kissing my brow and saying, "It will be all right, daughter. Let Me nurture your soul." The psalm spoke of the dark place I'd been in for so long, and the fierce anger of the Lord toward those who held me there. It reminded me of His blessed deliverance:

I will love thee, O Lord, my strength.
The Lord is my rock, and my fortress, and my deliverer;

my God, my strength, in whom I will trust;
my buckler, and the horn of my salvation, and my high
tower.
I will call upon the Lord, who is worthy to be praised:
so shall I be saved from mine enemies.
The sorrows of death compassed me, and the floods of
ungodly men made me afraid.
The sorrows of hell compassed me about: the snares of
death prevented me.
In my distress I called upon the Lord, and cried unto my
God:
he heard my voice out of his temple, and my cry came
before him, even into his ears.
Then the earth shook and trembled; the foundations
also of the hills moved
and were shaken, because he was wroth.
There went up a smoke out of his nostrils, and fire out
of his mouth devoured: coals were kindled by it.
He bowed the heavens also, and came down: and
darkness was under his feet.
And he rode upon a cherub, and did fly: yea, he did fly
upon the wings of the wind.
He made darkness his secret place; his pavilion round
about him
were dark waters and thick clouds of the skies.
At the brightness that was before him his thick clouds
passed, hail stones and coals of fire.
The Lord also thundered in the heavens, and the
Highest gave his voice; hail stones and coals of fire.
Yea, he sent out his arrows, and scattered them;
and he shot out lightnings, and discomfited them.
Then the channels of waters were seen, and the
foundations of the world
were discovered at thy rebuke, O Lord, at the blast of
the breath of thy nostrils.
He sent from above, he took me, he drew me out of

many waters.
He delivered me from my strong enemy, and from them
which hated me:
for they were too strong for me.
They prevented me in the day of my calamity: but the
Lord was my stay.
He brought me forth also into a large place; he
delivered me, because he delighted in me.

(Psalm 18:1-19, KJV)

"When I first got out I was very, very cautious about what I read, heard preached or taught, and believed. I checked it all with the Bible. As time has gone on I have become more comfortable with trusting the Holy Spirit and the check He gives me in my spirit when I read something or hear a teaching. I have also learned to trust my church and my pastor. It took many years, but I now feel very safe and secure there. If I'd done that before I got involved with Seth's group, I never would have gotten involved."

Expect triggers.

Whether you lived in a cult for a year or a decade, certain things happened over and over. Phrases and words used in specific ways twisted Scripture to suit the purposes of the leader. In some groups, even smells and sounds (specific incense fragrances, bells, and patterned hand-claps) may be used to condition followers' responses. Hearing, seeing, or experiencing something similar to what you went through can trigger a memory so strong it almost knocks you over. Knowing flashbacks not only can but will happen takes some of the terror out of it and enables you to become objective to quiet your emotions. You can step back and say, "Wow! What triggered that?" Evaluate the experience, and much of the fear will dissipate.

Jennifer: "I used to have extreme anxiety, even in church, when I hear Scriptures that Seth twisted and hurled at me in the cult. It made me ask myself, *Was he right?* As I continued to listen, I saw the truth, but the fear used to crop up. The flashback to the time when I believed God hated me and wanted to hurt me could be immobilizing, but I fought through it. Another area I used to really struggle with was when people came to pray for me. Naturally, they put a hand on my arm or shoulder. I found myself praying, 'Lord, I trust You that nothing will transfer into me.' It was so ingrained in my thinking and a real fear. Today, the fear comes back occasionally but it has definitely gotten better. I continue to press back against it to this day."

Be ready to fight.

Soldiers spend a lot of time in training, so that when they are called on to fight they can respond immediately. Ex-cult members will have issues to fight through, and should expect the challenge. Being aware the struggle will come is an advantage.

Jennifer: "Ten years have passed, and I still find it hard to read the Bible. Seth perverted verses, and then forbid us to read anything except Jesus' words or the book of 1 John. I bought a new Bible as one of my first acts of independence after leaving the cult. That helped somewhat. But I spent ten years not studying the Bible properly, not using it as the Sword of the Spirit it is meant to be. I've had to re-learn how to get my Sword out of its scabbard and use it in spiritual battle, just like a new Christian. Getting plugged into a solid, Bible-teaching church and surrounding myself with strong Christian friends and counselors has helped a great deal, but the final effort to actually read and internalize the Bible for myself is work I must do on my own."

Ask God to help.

He's watched over you along the deceptive path you've taken, longed for you to come home, and orchestrated things to make it possible for you to get out of the cult you're in. He won't abandon you now. Even if you don't feel comfortable telling other people about what you've been through, God already knows it, and He's ready to have you tussle it out with Him as you work through your issues and hurts. Don't let your past painful experience cut you off from the Source of your strength. Go to Him whenever you need strength for the next step on the path of recovery.

If you are concerned for someone who wants to exit a cult, or has already come out of one, your role is pivotal in his or her eventual recovery. Some people recover quickly, or at least make good progress early on. Jennifer and her mother were open and honest about their experiences, which helped their transition back into normal life and healing. Others can take ten years or more to heal; some never do.

One of the most pernicious things about cults and aberrant churches is that those wounded by them have a high likelihood of never regaining their spiritual equilibrium or trust in God and His people again. They abandon the church and either retreat into isolation or may even fall into another cult. Having friends who are realistic, knowledgeable, and willing to walk with them on the difficult road to spiritual recovery can spell the difference between success and failure.

Comparing Notes

I squeeze Gary's hand as we approach the front door of Afnan's home. Seeing her will be wonderful, now that we are both out of the cult, but I know Gary will no doubt hear some details this evening that he's not heard before. It will be tough for his loving heart to absorb them.

The door is flung open, and Afnan's high-voltage smile lights the air. Her long curling tresses frame an olive complexion, punctuated with lively brown eyes. We embrace. Gary shakes hands with Chris. Baby Elijah wiggles in Afnan's arms, confused but excited by all the activity.

"I'm so glad you're here!" Af draws us into the fragrant house. Her slightly deep voice, accented by her Middle Eastern heritage, has a musical quality. She passes the baby to Chris. "I have to go stir things in the kitchen."

I follow her to the room from which delicious steam carries exotic spices throughout the house. The sweetness of anise brushes the picklish pungency of coriander and mouth-watering meat sizzling in olive oil.

"You've gone to so much trouble." I survey the counters jammed with bowls, the sink filled with soaking pans, and the exquisitely set table in the adjoining dining area.

"I want you to taste my home." Afnan laughs. "I bet you've never had food like this, but I grew up on it in Israel. I wanted to celebrate."

"We can't wait to taste it. It smells awesome!"

As my friend flutters among the cooking dishes, I study her for signs of the struggles I still experience in the aftermath. Though there is the frantic nervousness of a hostess wanting to get everything right for her guests, I also sense the same peace that has come to me in a year and a half of healing.

Within a few minutes, the dining room sideboard is laden with aromatic platters of meat, vegetables, and interesting salads. Elijah reigns at one end of the table in his high chair, and we adults grow silent as the wondrous food claims all our attention. Afnan explains each dish—what is wrapped in the grape leaves, the special spice in the meat, the light and pungent cheese on the eggplant. Laughter adds an additional sweetener to the meal.

How different from where we both were just a couple of years ago. I picture solitary meals when I was forbidden to eat with my own mother. Even when we violated the rule, the meal never seemed to sit well with either of us. And nothing like this feast was ever on the menu.

I look longingly at Elijah in his chair, banging his little fist against the tray for more attention and more food. The ache in my heart is only softened slightly by the obvious joy on the faces of Afnan and Chris as they enjoy his antics. My empty arms and violated womb throb with regret.

The meal is untouched by talk of the past. That can wait until later.

* * *

I sink into the soft couch and recline against Gary's protective chest, as Chris and Afnan join us in the living room. The change of venue seems to bring with it a change in mood. Talk turns reflective, and cult memories spill out.

"We didn't know each other well, but we knew about each other," Afnan says, pulling her dark hair into a pony tail and fanning her hot neck, then dropping the hair back into place. "Seth kept us separated, but he would tell me that you were being very spiritual. It was a way for him to make me obey."

I gasp. "He told me the same thing about you!" I shake my head. "Whenever I wouldn't manifest demons like he wanted, or I couldn't do other things he demanded, he'd tell me that you seemed to have no problems with it, and you were making much better progress than I ever would."

Af's brown eyes meet my hazel gray ones and lock. I shiver a little, and Gary takes my hand.

"I don't see how he kept you both from walking away, especially if you didn't live together." Chris rubs his chin, shakes his head. "He seems so evil to me."

Afnan puts Elijah in his bouncy chair on the floor. "But he wasn't evil in the beginning. At first, he seemed like someone who was just very spiritual and had some answers to questions I couldn't figure out." She smiles into the baby's eyes and touches his cheek. "It was only later that he got weird."

"But what made you stay even when he got weird?" Chris leans forward and rests his elbows on his knees. He and Gary exchange a glance. It's clear they are both still struggling to understand our experience.

"Because he prophesied over me about so many things, and it was really exciting to think those things could happen. Though some of them I really doubted. Like saying I would get back together with my ex-boyfriend and he would be a great spiritual man in the future."

I choke on my iced tea. Gary, concerned, pats my back.

"Oh, my gosh. He said the same thing to me! He said my ex-husband—the one he'd told me to divorce—would come back to me when the prophetic time was right and would become a great man of God, and we'd have this tremendous ministry!"

Our eyes meet again.

"Interesting." Gary nods. "By keeping everyone separate in the group, he could go on using the same phony prophecies for each of you, and you'd never know it. Makes it easier for him if he doesn't have to keep making up new ones."

Silence falls like smoke, smothering conversation for a moment. Elijah's squeal of delight over a toy breaks the spell.

"Seth was always saying I had idols in my life and I had to get rid of them," Afnan said. She twirls a lustrous lock of shoulder-length black hair around her index finger. "He said my hair was an idol. It was almost to my waist, and I was proud of it. He made me cut it off."

My hands close over my abdomen. "He said my idol was that I wanted to be a mother so badly." My eyes stray to Elijah, then dart away. "He prayed over me to break the hold of that dream on me, and made me renounce it." My voice fades, and Gary's arm around my shoulders tightens.

"I remember the last time he beat me. He'd found out I'd made a friend outside the group—Chris—and said I had to cut off the relationship immediately. He kept hitting me and saying I could never see Chris again. I refused and told him to get out of my apartment." She slides her hands up and down her arms as though the bruises were still there. "He said if he left, I'd never see him again. I'd go to hell, and take Chris and everyone else I had contact with right to hell with me. 'Is that what you want?' he asked. I said, 'Get out.' He slammed out the door. I went straight to Chris and never saw Seth again."

"Do you wonder what you'd do if you saw him?" My question brings sparks to Afnan's eyes.

"I know exactly what I'd want to do—punch him!"

I lean into the warmth of Gary's subtle embrace and listen to the rage, the conviction, the sureness of Afnan's response. "We're free now; that's what matters."

My smile is slow but genuine. "And we're never going back."

* * *

From the outside looking in

IT'S HARD TO SAY whether I would have left Seth earlier if he'd run a traditional cult in which all the members were kept together continually. Afnan and I were surprised to discover so many things were used to manipulate both of us independently—and we're sure he used them on others. Perhaps he continues to do so today. Had we been able to compare notes while still in the cult, it might have brought understanding sooner. Perhaps. But we both made conscious choices throughout our experience and have had to come to grips with that fact.

Until now, you've been reading my story from my point of view. But what did my life look like from the outside? Could anybody tell my mother and I were under the influence of someone who was not interested in our welfare?

Here are stories from different points of view.

Laura—Coworker at the Diner

I met Ruth my first day working at the diner. Although Jen lived deep inside her, I didn't meet that woman for a very long time. At first she seemed just like anyone else. But, with time, I realized Ruth was anything but regular.

I liked Ruth right away. Kind and motherly, she took me under her wing, always taking time to show me how to do things and where to find everything. It seemed to come naturally to her. I would've assumed she had children had she not told me otherwise. Ruth told me she was a Christian in one of our very first conversations. She seemed excited to find out that I was a fellow believer and the daughter of a preacher. I was not living a Christian life at the time but still considered myself religious. I loved God but wasn't willing to sacrifice my life to His will. At nineteen I thought I had much better things to do with my time.

Even though I wasn't living the life I should, I had been raised in church my whole life, always around Christians who loved the Lord with all their heart. I could tell right away if someone's life showed spiritual fruit or not, even though there wasn't any in mine. So Ruth was an enigma to me. She talked about loving the Lord with zest and excitement, but I could still sense something very off; there was a dark place she wouldn't let me into.

As time went on, we became closer. I definitely considered her one of my friends. I noticed, though, that she never shared much about herself. It dawned on me that I did most of the talking and she listened. I told her all sorts of things about my life, but she never seemed to share much of her own story.

■ There was a dark place she wouldn't let me into. ■

As we grew closer, she opened up a little more and told me about her "father" and "mother," the pastors of the deliverance ministry she was involved in. I had seen many ministries in my life, yet I had never heard the term deliverance ministry. I found it very odd that she called her pastors "mother" and "father," especially because her birth mother worked with us as a waitress at the diner—something I didn't realize for weeks, because she called her mother "Marian." Referring to fellow believers as brother or sister so-and-so is typical in a church family, but never "father" or "mother." When I asked her about it, she explained that they were her spiritual parents, as if it were completely normal. She further informed me that Ruth was not her real name, but rather one her "father" had given her. She told me it represented her new life in Christ and that the old person she was had passed away. That was the first time I sensed something strange was going on.

As the months passed, I found out a lot more about Ruth, her mother, and their "ministry." I realized they gave all their money to the ministry and her "parents." Suddenly it made sense to me why Ruth worked day and night shifts week after week. Shocked, I called my mother to ask what she thought about the whole situation. She said she thought it a little odd, but maybe they were involved in a very small church. All churches (big or small) are financed with nothing but tithes, offerings, and donations. After speaking with my mother, I decided to leave it alone. I figured, "It's their life; it's none of my business." As it turned out, that was only the tip of the iceberg.

I rededicated my life to the Lord and became more intimate with my Savior. That choice made a big difference in my life. There wasn't a person at work who didn't notice the change, including Ruth, She was proud of me, and it made me feel good. As I grew closer to Him and studied the Word, more red flags rose in my mind about Ruth's life.

Many of her "father's" teachings did not stand up to the Word of God. I finally made up my mind. My friend was involved in a cult, not a ministry.

Over time, Ruth changed for the worse. She looked tired and worn down, not the slender, attractive, and sweet-faced woman I had originally met. She no longer wore makeup of any kind. She appeared to be tired physically, mentally, spiritually, and emotionally. When I would ask her why, she told me it couldn't be helped; she had no choice. She said she had to stay up studying or reading her Bible. "I have to be hard on myself until I get it. I'm still a horrible person."

It was obvious that she didn't have an accurate understanding of God's love or forgiveness in her life. She thought she only deserved punishment, discipline and wrath. I later found out that her so-called father would keep her on the phone all night. In these nightlong sessions he would verbally abuse her, tear her down, and continue his calculated brainwashings. I believe those were some of the most powerful tools he used to control her. She wasn't on the phone with a mere man—there were demons at work.

One morning Ruth and her mom came in, looking worn down. Ruth made the mistake of saying how tired she was, to which I replied, "Grab a cup of coffee; that'll help." She said they both were giving up coffee. They didn't want to, but they had to for the Lord. Naturally, I thought sarcastically. I knew her "father" had ordered it to keep them in a zombie state, to further instill the control and fear.

When things started to take a turn for the worse, Ruth had to gain weight. Everyone at work noticed this strange behavior because she paid close attention to her weight, focused on her health, and discussed every new diet craze with the rest of us girls. This was clearly out of character, but what could we do? Those were some of the hardest days to witness. The more weight she gained, the more any little bit of dignity she had left slipped away. She became a shell of a person-lost, lonely, hurting, and insecure in every area of her life.

The Holy Spirit put urgency on my spirit to pray for her. I did so daily, but I knew she wouldn't let me in yet. I prayed that the Holy Spirit would tell me exactly what to pray for her and He did-separation. I sensed it to be life or death that she leave the cult or otherwise separate from her "father" and "mother." I told everyone in my family to pray for her.

■ She became a shell of a person-lost, lonely, hurting, and insecure in every area of her life. ■

Not long after I started covering Ruth and Marian in prayers, Ruth came in to the diner with a cast on her hand. She also had clear bruise marks in the shape of fingerprints on her upper arms. She didn't have to speak a word to me; I knew who did this to her. It was written all over her face. Shame followed her like a dark shadow. I knew better than to ask her what had happened. I couldn't bear to hear whatever pitiful lie she had to come up with. Almost immediately, someone too loudly questioned, "What happened to your arm?!" She grimaced and gave the excuse of being clumsy and falling over a table.

They bought it! No one questioned any further. She covered up for that monster, a man who had somehow snaked his way in and made these women believe him their savior. Even a regular customer, a pastor, had no inkling of what it all meant. I was blown away! I thought for sure he would sense in his spirit what was going on, but he didn't. I felt like the only sane person in the diner that day.

That week I saw and sensed the overwhelming fear eating at Ruth. She was afraid and had to tell someone. She started fully opening up to me for the first time in the years I had known her. I praised and thanked God under my breath. It's about time!

Though still a bit guarded, it was clear she wasn't fooled anymore. Her senses began coming back to her; she knew what had happened to her was wrong. She began asking me lots of questions about what I believed and told me outrageous things her "father" was teaching and doing. I had no idea how gruesome some of the details were going to be. Her life had been a living hell.

In the end, Ruth and her mother cut ties with every aspect of the cult. I was one of a small group that accompanied them to move some of the household items that belonged to the cult leaders out of Ruth and Marian's house and into a storage unit. The place they had been ordered to live in by Seth felt thick with demonic power. Growing up as a minister's daughter had prepared me for the situation. I had come into contact with demon-possessed people in the past. An overwhelming presence of fear hit me when I entered the house. The evil presence made my skin crawl. We prayed in Jesus' name, commanding the demons to leave. The presence left and we completed our task. It was a frightening experience, and only a taste of the nightmare Ruth had lived with for ten years.

■ The evil presence made my skin crawl. ■

The next day I met Jennifer for the very first time, much like the original Ruth, yet better. I met the real her. The chains of the cult that had shackled her were no longer there. Her eyes held real light. She smiled, and the love of God was all over her. You could feel the freedom in her spirit; she was clearly a new creation. The little diner that had once been a prison for her slave labor now became a sanctuary and one of the things the Lord used to deliver her.

As Jen reclaimed her life and grew in the Lord, it was clear to me why the devil had worked so hard to stifle her. Jen is very special. She is a soul winner for the Lord. She clearly has an anointing on her life and touches everyone she meets in a very special way. The enemy worked very hard to keep her from reaching her full potential. For every misery Jen went through, God has replaced it with a blessing. I am so thankful God blessed me with Jennifer as a friend. He used her for great growth in my life and in my walk with him. I am proud to say that we are still friends to this day and watching her transformation has been a blessing and an honor.

"What do you think? If a man owns a hundred sheep and one of them wanders away, will he not leave the ninety-nine on the hills and go to look for the one that wandered off? And if he finds it, I tell you the truth, he is happier about that one sheep than about the ninety-nine that did not wander off." (Matthew 18:12-13, NIV)

Grace and Ira Weaver-Post-cult Prayer Counselors

"I remember there was a darkness in Jen's face—though Ira and I knew her as Ruth then. We'd see her and Marian at the diner, and they were both always very serious. They'd take customers' orders and dash away, never looking anyone in the eye. There was a real sense of oppression over both of them, but we didn't know what it was. I did sense it was spiritual, however."

Grace and Ira joke that they returned to the diner over and over for the oversized portions of haddock that kept appearing on his plate, but it was also an opportunity to keep in touch with the two women. "They were so clearly hurting." The Weavers love to joke, and it was difficult not to be drawn in by their warmth and friendliness. Ruth and Marian fought their kindness because they were so afraid they'd condemn them to hell or that demons would jump from them. Rather than their behavior pushing Ira and Grace away, it led them to pray for Ruth and Marian instead.

"Ruth would have bruises or a black eye, and then there was the broken hand. I felt almost like the devil was trying to hurt her through someone. I gave her my card, hoping some day she'd call me. It was a small thing, but I wanted to reach out to her without scaring her away."

Grace had no idea of the true gravity of the situation when Jen called her and said they needed help.

"When the two of them first came to talk to us, we could see they were very frightened. Seth had them convinced that by leaving the cult they were hell bound, and so were we, just for talking to them. We immediately began to speak truth back to them to counteract the lies."

The first session with Ira, Grace, and the other counselors was as traumatic for them as for Jen and Marian. When the two women spilled the story, the prayer team knew immediately this was something far bigger than they'd expected and realized why the two women had acted as they did for so long. The bondage of their hearts and minds was cunningly done and difficult to sever.

■ The bondage of their hearts and minds was cunningly done and difficult to sever. ■

"It's totally amazing to Ira and me—the whole prayer team, really—that they have made such huge progress." Since October 2007, when Jen and her mother made the break, they have embraced the process of healing. As Grace puts it, "They wanted everything God had for them. They sucked it right out of us and asked for more."

As the years slip by, it becomes easier to put aside the lies when they rear up again. Jen, Marian, Janice, Marian's sister, and Afnan all say they have very vivid nightmares still, and sometimes awake to almost sense the presence of Seth and Rhoda. This, too, is diminishing over time.

They were broken people when they abandoned Seth and his group. Financially, they could hardly be in worse shape. Seth and Rhoda had run up large bills on their credit cards and taken all the money they'd earned for nearly ten years. Physically, both were run down due to odd dietary rules and insufficient sleep. Jennifer's forced weight gain added to her physical misery and poor self-esteem. Emotionally, their ability to make decisions had atrophied to the point they were nearly paralyzed with fear.

Jen was frightened of Seth pursuing them and punishing them for leaving. She drove with one eye on the rearview mirror for a long time. He'd threatened to kill her if she ever left—when she'd been pregnant, that threat had extended to the baby. He'd managed to kill the baby through the coerced abortion; why should she think she could escape him?

As the truth of the Scriptures and the reality of God's love permeated Jen and Marian's minds and hearts, they realized Seth was no more than a man. "We have a heavenly Father to turn to for protection jand direction. We don't need someone to tell us what to eat, when and where to eat it, where to sit, what to do with every moment of the day and night. God's will is so much simpler and relaxed than all that! He wants us to love Him, accept that He loves us and forgives our sin, and trust Him to guide us throughout the rest of our lives."

Grace knew they were breaking free just by looking at them. "Their faces changed when they left the cult. People could clearly see something was different. Both of them began to walk differently, make eye contact, smile, and laugh. A light shone in their faces that wasn't there before."

■ A light shone in their faces that wasn't there before. ■

Ira is certain a major factor in Jen's recovery has been the steady love of her husband, Gary. "I don't know any other man who could support her in the condition she was in and all she had to deal with, other than Gary." Initially, Ira and Grace put the brakes on the relationship because they knew how fragile Jennifer was. But when they got to know Gary and he shared his heart concerning his desire to only do what was best for her, they saw God's hand in the timing of the relationship. Getting Ira's blessing was very special to Jen. "Seeing Gary's heart turned my initial concern around. He has been a significant factor for Jennifer's recovery and growth."

Acquaintances and Strangers

One of the prayer team counselors was surprised to hear Jen and Marian were allowed to go to work every day, go to stores, be out in the community. "It made me wonder how many people I come into contact with every day who are in a situation as abusive as this one was, and I don't see it," she said.

Going out—even to work—was fraught with stress. Jen spent time before leaving the house binding everything she could possibly imagine might be waiting for her in the world. The car had to be anointed if someone else had driven it. Conversation and interaction had to be kept to a minimum in all situations, even with coworkers, to avoid developing soul ties and risking the devil's intrusion into her life. When she left a place, there were specific prayers to pray to cut all such ties again.

This internal dialogue was invisible. What others saw was a person who was quiet to the point of being unfriendly, reserved to the point of rudeness, perhaps stuck up and proud. "I was not fun to be around, so a lot of people ignored me or had as little to do with me as possible in the course of a work shift. Being generally outgoing and friendly, this was painful for me. Yet I felt they were all harboring demons of one kind or another and I had to protect myself." Odd behavior generally doesn't scream "cult member" to those not educated in the signs of such involvement.

A few outsiders did try to break through, such as the landlords who sent Marian and Jen a letter saying they thought Seth was controlling them, and they'd help if the women wanted them to do so. "I couldn't risk Seth learning of their letter, so I told him about it myself. After he'd made me burn it, he insisted I go to their house and tell them off. I had to be mean, offensive, and belligerent. We moved within days of that encounter. My reaction to their overture obviously confirmed their suspicions, but they had no idea where we went after leaving their rental house and could not reach out to us except through prayer. It bothered me to be so awful to them, and it was such a delight and relief when I asked their forgiveness later and they extended it freely."

■ Odd behavior generally doesn't scream "cult member" to those not educated in the signs of such involvement. ■

Though injured regularly by Seth, Jennifer was never allowed to seek medical help. Red flags that might have gone up among nurses and doctors were thwarted this way. "My only hospital visit was toward the end when my hand was broken, and I had to have it set. By then I was very good at telling a story to cover what had caused my injury and escaped detection."

In short, though both Marian and Jennifer mingled with other people on an almost daily basis, there was nothing about them that gave anyone undeniable proof they needed to be extricated from a cult. There was something "odd" and "different" about the two, but because it was the two of them, and they were related, many people probably put it down to family social traits.

If you suspect someone is involved in an abusive group or cult, pray for him or her. Ask God for wisdom, insight, opportunities to interact. If at all possible, be like Ira and Grace: stay in touch, reach out any way you can, be available. You may be the only lifeline that person has when the time comes to make a move.

"I thank God for the people who reached out to us."

■ Thinking It Through. ■

Can't Somebody Help Me?

Whether you are caught in a spiritually abusive relationship or an actual cult, the sense of isolation that comes from cutting yourself off from society is profound. Jennifer and her mother were fortunate that they had people eager to help them, despite nearly a decade of silence on their part. For others, it can be a lonely journey from discovering the truth of the situation they're in, executing an escape plan, and taking the first steps in a multi-year healing process.

Many people have a heart for others in spiritually abusive situations. Some have been there themselves and want to offer assistance out of their own experience. Others simply see the need and have put resources into motion to help.

If you have been wounded by a spiritually deceptive person or organization, even if it was long ago, you don't have to walk alone. Others have tread the path you are on and are willing to listen, pray, advise, and extend the heart of God to you as you seek to get back on track once more.

Anti-Cult and Spiritual Deception
Recovery Organizations

Anti-cult and recovery ministries sometimes specialize in a particular type of deception (for instance, reaching out to people leaving one particular group, etc.), but most of them keep in touch with other groups and can direct you if they are not able to meet your needs.

Note: Websites and email addresses change continually, so we've not listed those contacts here. For the most current list, please visit our website: www.JenniferRedcay.com. You can also Google these ministries to get up-to-date contact information.

Ministries

- Watchman Fellowship, David Henke
- Christian Ministries International, Ron Carlson
- Saints Alive in Jesus, Ed Decker
- International Cultic Studies Association, Michael D. Langone
- New Life Ministries, Stephen Arterburn
- Spiritual Abuse Recovery, Jeff VanVonderen
- Reasoning from the Scriptures Ministries, Ron Rhodes
- Spiritual Abuse.org, Lois Gibson
- Berean Call, founded by the late Dave Hunt
- Biblical Discernment Ministries
- Christian Apologetics & Research Ministry
- Christian Research Institute, Hank Hanegraaff
- Cult Information Service
- Evangelical Ministries to New Religions
- Evangelical Outreach, Dan Corner
- Focus on the Faulty, Jay Howard
- MacGregor Ministries
- Spiritual Counterfeits Project

Chapter 10

Back to the Cult

I'm in the cult. Again.

I approach a table, order pad in hand, and duck my head. I must avoid eye contact at all costs. The couple at the table is familiar. Ira and Grace smile and try to get me to really see them. I fight the urge to smile.

I smell frying onions from the kitchen area, catch a glimpse of the green and white decor as I move between tables, hear the sound of the door as it opens and another customer enters. All my senses work to drag me back to my previous life as surely as if Seth's hand held my arm and clawed at my heart. My steps slow, and I can hardly believe I'm here. Again.

"Can't you look more upset?" Randy clutches his clipboard and coaches me through my first (and, I hope, last) acting job. He and the rest of the crew from *The 700 Club* television program have come to document my story, film snapshots of my life in the cult and afterward, and give me the opportunity to warn others about the dangers of spiritual abuse.

"The problem is that you're glowing too much." Ira grins and straightens his water glass for another take.

"I'm trying. It's really difficult. I don't feel the pain any more—it's like that person who was so sad was never me, as if I never felt it." I'm frustrated with my own inability to project what they need. I'm also delighted. When I cry these days, I weep tears of joy. I've come a long, long way.

*　*　*

Most people would never seriously consider reliving their worst life experiences in front of a camera. It's a lot harder than it looks on television. Today, while I go through the motions, my heart is free. It makes a world of difference.

As the film team sets up for another scene, Gary and I change clothes at the lovely home we are using as a set. The home is back in the woods, the windows are open, a breeze stirs the curtains, and sheep bleat in the nearby meadow. Peace drapes over me like lovely fog.

We step out onto the sun deck, and my heart catches in my throat. Everyone there loves me, and their warm support flows over me. My mother is grinning her high-wattage smile. Ira and Grace know their turn before the cameras is coming and look a little edgy. My newfound friend and sister in Christ, Jill, the owner of the house, and her three children are enjoying the fun of the shoot. My mind fills with my favorite phrase: *This is awesome.*

A crew member beckons and asks me to sit in a chair for the interview. Randy sits no more than six inches from me. My heart beats a bit faster as I work to control my automatic reaction to being so close to another person. I take a few deep breaths. The questions begin, and I relax as I frame the answers I hope will throw the spotlight on God and all He's done for me.

There is much I could share. Details flood my mind—the initial excitement of being prophesied over, the dank smell of the moldy house we lived in, the ringing of the phone at all hours to summon me to obedience, the blows from Seth's fists as he tried to make me compliant, the abject fear of hell should I disobey. Rather than these things, what I want most to convey can never be clear enough: God loves me. He kept track of me even in the cult. He led my mother and me out when the time was right and I was ready to go. He showered blessings upon me and restored my life in a gentle, loving, methodical way. There are not enough words to praise Him for all that.

* * *

"Now we'll shoot the Happy Couple scene." Randy looks up from his clipboard. "You and Gary walk along by the pond. Walk slowly. We need plenty of footage on this because there will be voice-over with it. Smile, laugh, enjoy the stroll."

Like children on a summer day, we join hands and amble down the bank. Gary squeezes my hand. An easy grin forms across my mouth. Maybe this is what real acting is about—feeling the scene and being part of it. I don't have to act happy. It bubbles out of both of us.

"Why don't you sit down there at the edge and put your feet in the water?" Randy's direction draws a quick inhale from Gary. He knows my past fears, my conditioning, the things I still fight to keep from controlling me. Feet-in-water was a definite no-no in the cult.

We get comfortable at the water's edge and I slide my feet into the water, splashing a bit. I enjoy the liquid coolness as it flows across my skin, swinging my feet to create small waves. Gary's smile grows as he sees me get past another mental roadblock. We giggle and carry on, almost forgetting the cameras are there.

* * *

The final scenes are the hardest. I'm asked to sit with my Bible, look confused, sad, in turmoil. With everyone standing around watching me, it's harder than the interview. I fall into my cult behavior too easily and begin rocking back and forth on the couch. I did that a lot during my ten years of bondage. At least they don't ask me to immerse myself in the role too long. My mother reminded me how I used to hit myself over and over, calling myself names. I'm glad I'd forgotten, and that I don't have to repeat it.

"I think we've got enough," Randy says at last. Crew members nod and begin to shut down equipment. As they clean up, we continue to talk about the after-effects of the cult on my life, especially our desire for children. One of the camera people asks if she can pray for me, and the whole group gathers in a circle. We hold hands and the day ends as I realize I have made new friends. We were strangers at the beginning of the day, but because of the connection we have in Christ, it seems we've known each other for years.

I don't try to stop the tears.

* * *

The yellow brick road

WHERE DOES A PERSON GO after emerging from a decade of deception? What comes next?

Real life. Leaving a cult is the first step on a long road to spiritual peace, and it has plenty of bumps and potholes along the route. As I move forward into the rest of my life, I continue to deal with echoes of the past. Sometimes the echoes are soft and I ignore them; other times, they are so loud I'm amazed no one else hears them.

■ As I move forward into the rest of my life, I continue to deal with echoes of the past. ■

Gary and I hoped God would heal one area immediately: make me a mother again. The aching loss of my baby through coerced abortion causes my arms to long for a child. All I ever wanted when I was growing up was to be a wife and mother. Once I had completed my counseling with Ira and Grace, and then with my post-abortion counselor, we began to pray I'd become pregnant.

Some minor corrective surgery for me made us hopeful I could be thankful in a new way by Thanksgiving 2009. But the holidays came and went...and my heart flowed out with them. We talked to a fertility specialist.

Conception treatments are incredibly expensive. The tests are invasive, humiliating, and time-consuming. Medications are as expensive as rare gems. We went through two rounds of treatments—more than we could afford—and then faced the fact that in this area, God's sovereignty would have to be accepted. In my mind, I felt the healing of this one part of my experience in the cult would be the trigger to release the entire cult nightmare from my mind and heart forever. God, however, sees farther and deeper than we do, and He knew I had to work through the issues of guilt and shame, not just move on to a new phase and try to forget.

The word adoption cropped up in our conversation more frequently once we'd given up on having our own biological child. We soon learned it is expensive and can take many years. Nonetheless, we began paperwork to demonstrate our ability and willingness to become parents.

Hungry to love a child and hopeful we might make a difference in a young life, we also began foster parent training. It would be wrenching to have children come and go from our home, but we also felt it was something God wanted us to do. I needed to open my heart to give and receive love freely, and children have a magical way of encouraging that.

■ I needed to open my heart to give and receive love freely. ■

We hoped to foster a baby. Perhaps he or she would become available for adoption down the road. Though I was tempted to fret about the delay, the possibilities, the potential for heartbreak, God's peace flowed over me and we were able to be patient. When we got a call about a seventeen-month-old little girl who needed foster parents immediately.

Letty's brown eyes were enormous. Her confused little bird expression took my breath away. We loved her immediately and completely. It seemed only a few hours after she entered our home that she'd been there all along. Gary and I would both creep in to watch her sleeping, enjoy the scent of a little one, and pray over her crib for her present and future.

God has plans within plans, and smiles at our attempts to stage direct our lives. We were overjoyed when we got the word that Letty was going to join our family and become a Redcay. At last, my arms were filled for good. And we've since been blessed with other children who have come to our home, hurting and sad. Some leave, and some may be taking the same road Letty did—into our home, into our hearts, into our forever family. We had no idea that God would turn my desire for children into a mission for Him.

Letty was our first adopted child, however God had other plans. We have since had the pleasure of adopting 4 other children from the foster system. Their lives were in complete chaos when they entered our home. But with the gentle touch of our Father, they are healing. They had so many hurts from their past but God is applying His balm of Gilead and we are seeing them start to recover. My experience in the cult has actually help me to be a safe place of healing for them. I understand what it feels like to be abused and broken but I also know what it feels like to be healed. Jesus knew they needed me as much as I needed them.

God does restore "the years the locusts have eaten" (Joel 2:25, NIV) but in unexpected ways. He can't go back and make me twenty-six again, the age when I entered the cult. But He has helped me grow up at last, take responsibility for my actions, and take joy in the age I am today. My ex-husband married someone else after we divorced. But God brought Gary into my life to bring the smile back to my face and healing to my heart. He also allowed me to have closure and even blessing from my ex-husband in our conversation on the phone after I came out of the cult.

I used to struggle daily with reverberations of false teaching. But God used that to keep me vigilant, stokes my hunger for the Word, and arms me to help others fight against the blinding terror of spiritual oppression.

Deep wounds leave scars. I will wear my scars for life, but I'm in good company: Jesus wears His scars, too.

* * *

After my initial fear subsided of seeing Seth or possibly being pulled back to the group, my righteous anger surfaced. Part of my counseling included accepting responsibility for things that happened to me, but not everything was my fault. Some things Seth inflicted on me against my will, and he was wrong. I didn't know what to do about that.

"This guy should be in jail," more than one friend told me. "Why don't you turn him in?"

The question intrigued and intimidated me. Obviously, in order to bring a complaint against Seth I would have to tell the whole story to a complete stranger. And, if it came to charges and an arrest, I'd have to tell it again. And again. And again.

Gary and I discussed whether it was worthwhile even thinking about it. It would be painful and embarrassing.

"We don't even know if it's actionable," Gary reasoned. "At least we could talk to a police officer and get his feedback."

Gary's willingness gave me courage. We made an appointment to see an officer and began to pray for wisdom in how to tell the story, what to emphasize.

If you have been in an abusive group and are considering reporting your abuser(s) to the police, keep the following tips in mind.[12]

- It is difficult to win cases in which you participated willingly in your own abuse and perhaps there were no witnesses. Even so, your "willingness" may have been coerced, and the proper attorney can bring that out.

- You must be clinical and blunt when you tell your story to an officer. Stick to facts that can be dealt with legally. *Tort* is the term for a crime that results in injury to another person and is prosecutable. Don't bog down telling a policeman about the religious heresy and spiritual problems of the group you were in. Talk instead about things that are illegal. I was beaten, sexually abused, and forced to undergo an abortion. These are things a court could take action on.

- Watch your language. The terms cult and brainwashing have loaded connotations. The abusiveness of the leaders of the group and the use of mind control or undue influence should be the focus. Make a written statement of the facts before you go and review it for all hot-button words that should be modified to keep the meeting on track.

- Check with your potential witnesses before you ever press charges. If others were involved in the cult with you, are they willing to testify? Can they look the leader in the eye in a courtroom? Do they have valuable information to add—or just sensationalism and religious differences? Have contact information with you when you meet the officer, in case he decides to investigate further.

- As much as possible, write down dates, places, and other details. Each time Seth took me to a motel and abused me, he told me to get rid of everything I had with me. Each of those nine times I replaced my driver's license is on record with the state. For me, that would be the beginning of a timeline necessary in any prosecution.

- Make sure you are able to endure the process for the long term. Is your family behind you? A case like this can take a long time to build and may go through many phases. If you don't have complete support from your spouse and family members, you may not be able to stick with it to the end.

- Even if your report doesn't generate a case and an arrest, it will accomplish something: It will put your abuser(s) on the police radar. Those who perpetuate spiritual abuse that leads to other types of harm usually do not suddenly wake up one day and stop their activities. Just because you left the group, even if the group seemed to fall apart later, does not remove the deceptive nature of the people in the organization. Getting the group and/or the leader on the record as a person to be aware of may do someone else good later.

Gary and I met with an officer in 2010. It was the first time Gary had heard every detail of my ordeal, and I know it affected him deeply. I told the officer about forced sexual encounters, the abortion, physical abuse, and more. The immediate problem of jurisdiction surfaced. Each time Seth had me take him to a motel, we went to a different county or township. Jurisdictional issues complicate any prosecution immeasurably. The abortion was performed in another state entirely, which raised a question as to whether the charges would be federal ones. In the end, the officer agreed to talk to the district attorney and prosecutor to try to unravel the issues of legal authority.

At this date of this book's writing, I have not heard further and have not pursued the issue. For me, great healing came in just telling the story to an unbiased listener who had some authority to determine if there were crimes committed.

The most sobering, alarming moment came when I had to identify Seth by his computerized driver's license photo. It sent a shiver down my back to see how angry and unpleasant Seth looked in the photo. If my eyes had been open wider all those years ago, perhaps that would have been enough to stop me.

They're open now, and I'm determined to continue pushing back the darkness, one day at a time.

■ Thinking It Through. ■

Taking Out Cult Insurance

An insurance salesman's first job is convincing the prospective customer that a need exists for his product. He might paint a grim picture of what a man's family would be like if he died suddenly in an accident without life insurance—how would the mortgage get paid, the kids go to college and the family be secure? Once he's caught the customer's attention, the sale is almost a foregone conclusion.

Cult proofing yourself, your family, and even your church is much the same process. You won't pay attention to the need if you don't realize it exists. Use the following tips to put together a good "anti-cult policy."

Acknowledge that cults exist, are probably operating right in your community, and that you could fall into one. While many people will accept the first two points of that statement, most refuse the third.

Margaret Thaler Singer, regarded as the world's "foremost authority on brainwashing,"[13] cited the reluctance to recognize one's own vulnerability as playing a key role in spiritual deception.

> "Just as most soldiers believe bullets will hit only others, not themselves, most citizens like to think that their own minds and thought processes are invulnerable. 'Other people can be manipulated, but not me,' they declare. People like to think that their opinions, values and ideas are inviolate and totally self-regulated. They may admit grudgingly that they are influenced slightly by advertising. Beyond that, they want to preserve a myth in which other persons are weak-minded and easily influenced, but they are strong-minded."[14]

Be aware of the warning signs—and heed them. If you read a road sign that says the bridge is out ahead and yet you keep driving, there should be no surprise about the outcome. Warning signs are meant to protect us, something true in regard to our mental and spiritual health, as well. Previous chapters in this book list warning signs to be aware of, how to discern truth from lies, and the devastating effectiveness of mind control techniques.

If you encounter an attractive church or organization, take your time getting to know people and exploring its doctrines and theology. If alarm bells or uneasiness occur for any reason, back up and evaluate why you reacted as you did. Do the doctrines square with the Bible? Is there an unhealthy amount of attention and devotion to the leader of the group? Do you sense an "us versus them" mentality with respect to other churches and organizations? Are you encouraged to put your mind in neutral and just accept certain things by faith "for now"? Is there an isolationist culture in which people seem to cling to others in the group to the exclusion of family, friends, coworkers, and others because they don't possess "the truth" espoused in the group?

If so, walk away. Better yet, run.

Cultivate stable relationships with spiritually mature believers. Cults draw in the unwary, tell them they are special, encourage them to keep this "deeper truth" to themselves and begin to control the person's life in short order. Don't give up friendships with people outside whatever church or organization you are involved in. Talk about what you're learning and compare notes. If you find yourself always making excuses for your group or perceive concern in the advice and tone of other Christians, re-evaluate.

Keep up your guard with further study. An athlete training for the Olympics does his or her routine over and over until it is second nature. When the crowd is roaring and the pressure is on, all the training comes into play. Think of your spiritual life as a routine that must be practiced and maintained. Read stories online or in magazines and books about people who have experienced spiritual deception. Make mental lists of the things that should have tipped off those who went astray and look for those same principles in your current experience. Train yourself so well to recognize the marks of spiritual deception that you react instinctively when you encounter them—as you inevitably will.

Talk to God about it. It's easy to turn personal cult insurance into mental gymnastics. It's a matter of the heart and the spirit and should be approached as such. Pray for guidance. Ask God to alert you to problems, guide decisions about where to worship (and with whom), and wait for His confirmation. You are precious in His sight, and He longs to see you walk the road of spiritual health and joy.

Epilogue

It would be easy to be bitter about losing ten years of my life to lies and deception, or to spend the rest of my life kicking myself for allowing it to happen. The thing about life is that it unrolls in only one direction: forward. It takes hard work to cling to the past, rather than embrace what God has in store down the road. I choose to learn from what happened and let it go.

It was an awful experience, but I would go through it all again—every day of those ten years—if I knew I'd come out of it at the end able to experience the love and forgiveness of God, as I do now and to have a personal relationship with Jesus and not religion.

Acknowledgments

To communicate the details of my experience was to relive the ten years I spent in abuse and bondage. As I recalled the past, it was so easy to feel the weight of the darkness again, but the evidence of God's light was overwhelming in the memories of breaking free.

To my husband, Gary, who continues to embody Christ's example of unconditional love in our marriage and in our family. Without your prayer and support my healing may not have been as complete. Apart from Jesus, you are my life—I love you!

I am forever grateful to Becca, my mentor, my friend and my partner in this book adventure. I am so thankful that she listened to the Holy Spirit that day in church and said yes when I asked her to write my story. I am so glad that the Lord picked you to be part of my healing

I am not sure I would have even lived through the abuse if it were not for my mother. You remained in bondage, only to try to save me. Thank you for continuing to search for the truth when I didn't have the strength to.

To Ira and Grace and the prayer team who led me through my counseling, thank you for your willingness to be used by the Lord to minister healing to the broken-hearted! Ira, I am so glad you loved the diner's haddock and kept coming back all those years. God is good!

Finally to my family who prayed me through all those years and did not give up! I love all of you.

Lastly to my Home Group—your encouragement and prayers are so cherished. I finally know what it means to have true friends! You are all such an amazing example of the body of Christ! Thank you.

JENNIFER REDCAY

* * *

Writing a book is a long and draining process. I was sustained through it by the grace of God, the encouragement of my wonderful husband, Bob, and the necessary correction of my critique partners: Vickie Phelps, Donna Paul, Pamela Dowd, and Nanci Huyser. Wilma Carr also pored over the manuscript to find last corrections, and put off her spring gardening to do it. I am blessed to have them all in my life.

I am indebted to Jennifer Redcay's friends, family members, and counselors, who took time to sit and talk with me about their experiences, sent lengthy emails of their impressions of her progress, and embraced us in this work with prayer and kindness. This book would not have come about, however, without Jennifer's utter commitment to transparency, honesty, and a willingness to face her past without flinching. It is her courage, and that of the others quoted in this book, that gives it power to transform lives.

I pray for all who read it, and I am eager to see it touch hearts and heal spirits. Jesus Christ can rebuild any life; just ask Jennifer.

BECCA ANDERSON

Notes

[1] MacArthur, John; "What is Biblical Discernment and Why is it Important?"; www.ondoctrine.com/2gty0301.htm; 2000, 2001.

[2] Steven Hassan, Combatting Cult Mind Control (Rochester, VT: Park Street Press, 1990), pp. 55-56.

[3] Edgar H. Schein, Coercive Persuasion, 1961 (The Massachusetts Institute of Technology, W.W. Norton, 1971), as quoted in Combatting Cult Mind Control, ibid., p 67.

[4] Robert J. Lifton, The Future of Immortality and Other Essays for a Nuclear Age (New York, Basic Books, 1987).

[5] www.abortionno.org, accessed August 7, 2010.

[6] Rachel K. Jones, Mia R.S. Zolna, Stanley K. Henshaw and Lawrence B. Finer, "Abortion in the United States: Incidence and Access to Services, 2005, www.gutmacher.org/pubs/journals/4000608.pdf, accessed August 16, 2010.

[7] www.abortionno.org, accessed August 10, 2010.

[8] Teri Reisser and Paul Reisser, A Solitary Sorrow (Colorado Springs, CO: WaterBrook Press), p. 173.

[9] Research by Mary K. Zimmerman in Passage Through Abortion, 1977, cited by Frederica Mathewes-Green in Real Choices (Ben Lomond, CA: Conciliar Press, 1997), p. 180.

[10] http://ramahinternational.org/post-abortion-syndrome-symptoms.html, accessed August 17, 2010.

[11] Ibid.

[12] Concepts taken in part from: Lawrence Levy, Esq., Prosecuting an Ex-Cult Member's Undue Influence Suit, Cultic Studies Journal, 1990, Volume 7, Number 1, pages 15-25, accessed via International Cultic Studies Association website, January 1, 2010).

[13] Steven Rubenstein, Kevin Fagan, San Francisco Chronicle, Tuesday, November 25, 2003.

[14] Margaret Thaler Singer, Ph.D., "The 'Not Me' Myth: Orwell and the Mind," www.rickross.com/reference/singer/singer4.html, accessed December 30, 2009.

About the Author

Jennifer Redcay spent 10 years of her young womanhood in a cult that nearly extinguished her soul, her spirit, her life. Though getting out of the cult was a glorious experience, it was only the beginning of a long road to recovery. She reaches out with joy and compassion to others who are in or could join similar groups. It is her passion to see others set free from bondage and all forms of abuse.

Today, Jennifer is happily married to Gary Redcay, and together they have adopted five beautiful children. In addition to their adopted children, they have three adult children and five grandchildren.

Jennifer welcomes reader comments and contact at www.JenniferRedcay.com

BECCA ANDERSON graduated with a degree in journalism and spent 20 years in public relations for agencies and corporations before becoming a full-time freelance writer and the editor of a business magazine in Canada. Becca understands the pressures, allure, and danger of cults from her own experience. Part of her personal recovery was to write the novel Shadow of Deceit (previously published as The Gathering Place). Since then, she has spent over 20 years researching cults, mind control, and spiritual abuse. Many people have shared their stories of similar experiences with her. If you would like to share yours, she would love to hear from you. Becca and her husband live in East Texas, where she is always storing away material for another book in some corner of her computer hard drive.

To email her: banderson@cablelynx.com
www.beccathewriter.com